The Little Book of Wicklow

THE LITTLE BOOK OF WICKLOW

CHRIS LAWLOR

The History Press Ireland

In memory of Fr Joe Whittle,
a Wicklow historian and an inspiration to me.

First published 2014

The History Press Ireland
50 City Quay
Dublin 2
Ireland
www.thehistorypress.ie

British Library Cataloguing in Publication Data.
A catalogue record for this book is available from the British Library.

ISBN 978 1 84588 856 5

Typesetting and origination by The History Press

CONTENTS

INTRODUCTION

Wicklow, a medium-sized Irish maritime county, 782 square miles in area, is unique, scenic and historic. Much of the interior of the county is made up of the large remote fastnesses of the Wicklow Mountains. These are some 500 million years old and were formed during the period of Caledonian folding, which produced the granite so synonymous with Wicklow today. Lugnaquilla, the highest mountain in the province of Leinster and one of the highest in Ireland, dominates the range, brooding silently over all else. Hill walking is popular in central Wicklow, but the landscape changes in both the east and west of the county. In the east, a fertile coastal plain provides an excellent location for the county's larger towns, all of which have maritime locations. In the west, rolling hills produce an undulating landscape with a patchwork of fields and farms, as the landscape becomes lower and eventually tails across the county boundary into the great central plain of Ireland.

While the natural beauty of Wicklow attracts many visitors, the county's heritage is also a significant factor for many tourists. There are many historic sites, such as Glendalough, Wicklow Gaol and the Dwyer-McAllister cottage, throughout the county. This book takes a look at some aspects of Wicklow's colourful history. It focuses both on what happened in the county and on the exploits of some of Wicklow's sons and daughters, many of whom excelled and were influential in various fields of human endeavour. The stories featured in this book range from the deeds of the great and the good to the misdeeds of the lesser and the bad. From saintly monks to vile murders, County Wicklow has seen it all over the centuries. Wicklow people have made history on land, sea and in the air, and this *Little Book of Wicklow* tries to capture some of that astonishing history. I hope you enjoy delving into the past of wonderful Wicklow!

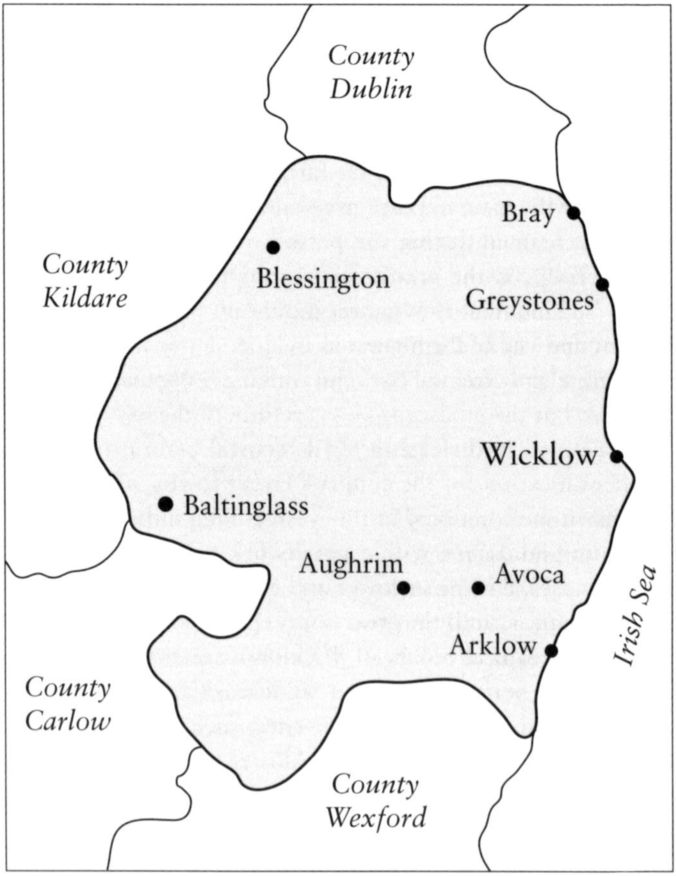

1

MONASTIC WICKLOW

County Wicklow has no shortage of monasteries, abbeys and priories, but one site stands head and shoulders above all others in terms of its monastic significance. Glendalough was one of the most important monasteries in Ireland, and its monastic community flourished right through Ireland's Golden Age, when the island was known as the Island of Saints and Scholars. This remote Wicklow valley was a huge centre of learning, power and influence during the early Middle Ages, both before and after the Norman conquest of Ireland.

GLENDALOUGH

Glendalough monastery lies in a glaciated valley, with its wide floor and steep sides. A waterfall cascades down from a hanging valley, flowing into a rock basin lake below. The name Glendalough actually means 'the valley of the two lakes': the rock basin lake has been divided in two by the alluvial fan below the waterfall. Hence Glendalough contains both an upper lake and a lower lake. The valley is set at the very heart of the Wicklow Mountains, and marks out the path of a long-vanished glacier as it travelled down from its birthplace in a corrie near the Wicklow Gap, and on into the lowlands beyond the village of Laragh.

ST KEVIN

The illustrious monastery sprang from humble beginnings. According to legend and folklore, St Kevin came from a wealthy and noble family of the Dal Mesincorb, one of the Irish royal tribes. He was a very solemn and pious youth who attended a well-known monastic school at Kilnamanagh, near Tallaght in County Dublin. Kevin desired from a young age to live in a place of solitude, where he could devote his life to God. He left Kilnamanagh and arrived in Hollywood in west Wicklow, where he established himself as a holy man. However, in order to escape the amorous advances of a local maiden named Kathleen, Kevin crossed the mountains, eventually arriving in the isolated and peaceful valley of Glendalough. According to the Irish annals, Kevin began his existence as a hermit in the valley about the year AD 530 by hiding himself in a hollow tree away from the gaze of others, to rid himself of all distractions. One would imagine that this wild man of the woods would be left severely alone, but this was not to be the case.

Kevin, it seems, worked a miracle by supplying milk for a herdsman's sickly child and the herdsman told everyone about the remarkable occurrence. Kevin's fame spread and he was recalled to Kilnamanagh by his superiors. He pursued further studies and was ordained by Bishop Lugidus. However, he pined for the solitude and simple life of Glendalough, and he eventually returned there, where 'he founded a great monastery in the lower part of the valley where the two rivers form a confluence'. Kevin's austere asceticism and general holiness attracted many followers, and the monastery began to grow. However, Kevin still yearned for solitude and so he left the running of the monastery to suitable men, appointing each of them to a separate religious position, before removing himself to the upper part of the valley of Glendalough to continue his hermit-like existence at Tempeall na Scellig, ordering his monks to leave him alone so that he could enter into a life of quiet contemplation and meditation while fasting in order to become closer to God. Kevin survived thus for a period of 7 years and, according to the *Annals of the Four Masters*, died on 3 June 618, aged 120 years (or 117 years if one reads the *Annals of Ulster*).

The great age attributed to Kevin is only one of a number of pointers which indicate that he was an extraordinary man. Legends abound regarding the saint and his holiness. From the very beginning, it seems, his life was punctuated by a number of remarkable and inexplicable occurrences, known collectively as the miracles of St Kevin. The first of these concerns the sudden change in the weather immediately following Kevin's birth. The extremely cold winter weather stopped suddenly and the whole countryside was immersed in balmy, mild spring weather for a continuous period of 7 years. When the infant Kevin was baptised by St Cronan, twelve immaculate white angels surrounded the baptismal font. Each angel held a lighted candle, all burning much brighter than any earthly light.

Kevin's choice of Glendalough as the site of his monastery is also the subject of a legend. When Kevin was looking for a site for his monastery, a goose flew in continuous circles around the valley of Glendalough to indicate the amount of ground that the local king should grant to Kevin for his new foundation. This is one of a number of legends in which Kevin is portrayed as communing with nature and having a special affinity with birds and animals. In fact, Kevin is something of an Irish St Francis of Assisi in this respect. Supposedly King Brandubh, when hunting a wild boar through the valley of Glendalough, came upon Kevin kneeling in prayer in the open, with many birds perched on his outstretched hands and arms. A similar story is told recounting how Kevin was at prayer one day when a blackbird landed on his hand and laid her eggs in his upturned palm. When the saint came out of his reverent trance-like state, he noticed the eggs and, rather than harm any of God's creatures, he remained in the same position for a number of weeks until the eggs were hatched and the fledglings had left the nest. A statue of Kevin in the church in Laragh village shows him with the blackbird's nest in his hand, recalling the episode.

Kevin was not quite so kind to all birds, however. He cursed the ravens of Glendalough and would not allow them to eat any meat during religious festivals and events held in his honour. The reason behind the saint's curse on the ravens is lost in obscurity, but the motive for his silencing the skylarks of Glendalough has come down to us through oral tradition. According to folklore, the workmen building the cathedral of Glendalough were becoming tired, weak and sickly because they would rise with the lark and lie down with the lamb. This gave them a very long and heavy working day, as the larks rose very early in the morning, creating untold hardships for the craftsmen and labourers employed on the building. Kevin had sympathy for the men and their plight, so he pleaded with God not to allow the larks to sing in Glendalough. The Lord heard Kevin's entreaty and granted his request, making the valley a place where, according to legend, no skylark ever sings. The opening lines of Thomas Moore's poem, *By that Lake whose Gloomy Shore* (1811), refer to this legend:

> By that lake whose gloomy shore, skylark never warbles o'er,
> Where the cliff hangs high and steep, young Kevin stole to sleep.

Kevin's love of nature was not confined to birds. Animals and even reptiles came under his spell as well. One legend recounts how Kevin was reading a valuable and rare vellum psalter when he lost his grip on the book and it fell into the lake below the saint's resting place. No sooner had the book disappeared below the surface of the water, however, than an otter surfaced from the silent depths, bearing the psalter on his nose. When the grateful saint retrieved the precious volume, he found that it was bone dry, despite having been fully immersed in the water. In another legend, Kevin was bathing in the lake when he was attacked by a serpent. Although the reptile managed to bite Kevin, he came to no harm – his skin was not punctured and the bite did not hurt him in any way.

Kevin's lakeside dwelling also meant that many legends regarding his daily journeys around and across the water were passed down orally through many generations. It was reported that Kevin, who used to say Mass in a small village on the far side of the lake from his own dwelling, often crossed the lake without using a boat – literally walking on water. On one occasion, he was praying and fasting at his cave during Lent when an angel appeared to warn him to move as a large rock was about to fall on his head. Kevin, however, refused to budge, as it would mean breaking his penitential Lenten observance, so the angel interceded with God on the saint's behalf. When Kevin rose and walked across the water after sundown on Holy Saturday (the eve of Easter Sunday), the rock immediately fell, leaving churning water in the wake of the saint when it tumbled from the rocky ledge above into the still waters below.

Other legends about St Kevin abound. One of these concerns a visiting sick friend of the saint who had an unusual craving for apples, as he believed they could cure him. Apples were out of season, and there was no apple tree near at hand, but Kevin picked three luscious apples from a willow tree beside the lake, and when his companion ate them, he was immediately cured. Kevin's generosity features in many of the stories, and in one instance the saint punished lack of generosity in another. One day he met a

woman carrying a basket covered with a cloth. Kevin asked her what she had in the basket and the sly dame told the saint that she was carrying stones, as she did not care to share her bread with a hungry man. Kevin recognised the lie for what it was and he retorted that if she had stones they would turn into bread, but if she had loaves of bread, they would turn into stones. Dismayed and ashamed, the woman threw away the stones that were now weighing her down, and these round stones can still be seen on the south side of the Lower Lake, between the monastic site and Rhefeart.

Yet another legend tells of how, when the monks at Rhefeart church were singing a hymn to St Patrick, the abbot told them to sing the hymn again and again. When they had done so three times, he enlightened them as to the reason for his request. Apparently he had seen a vision of St Patrick standing over them and holding a bishop's crozier while blessing the community during the singing. Visions of saints and angels were often attributed to Kevin, and when he eventually died it is said that hosts of angels filled the remote valley and lined up along the lakeside, singing and praising God. Pilgrims from all over Ireland and further afield who came to Glendalough in later times often wished to be buried in the shadow of the monastic ruins for the love of God and his holy angels as well as devotion to St Kevin himself.

MONASTIC RUINS

The monastic ruins in Glendalough are impressive indeed. Irish monasteries of the early Middle Ages were unlike the communal buildings of later medieval confraternities in continental Europe. European monks, who often lived according to the Rule of St Benedict, lived, worked and prayed together in one large monastery or abbey, but earlier Celtic Irish monasteries consisted of small individual dwellings. Every monk had his own small cell, and these were dispersed and dotted around with the churches and communal monastic buildings at the centre. Most of the buildings of the old monastery are no longer extant and the individual monks' cells and the huts of masons, smiths and craftsmen are long gone. Most of these were constructed of wood or wattle and daub. Wattle was the name given to small saplings, usually of willow or hazel wood, interwoven horizontally around a series of vertical wooden stakes driven into postholes in the ground. Daub was a wet mud used as plaster, which was used to cover the wattle, fill the cracks and keep out draughts. When the mud dried, it hardened and created a weatherproof wall. However, in the long term, wattle and daub – like wooden buildings – proved susceptible to the ravages of the weather over many centuries, so these buildings no longer exist at Glendalough. What remains today are the ruins of the stone buildings that stood at the centre of the once-proud monastic city.

The monastic city was accessed via the great stone gateway. This consisted of two arches, both undecorated (about 9½ feet wide and 2½ feet thick), enclosing an interior gatehouse space of approximately 16 square feet. This was paved with large, rough floor slabs. On the right hand side as one enters through the gateway, one of the slabs in the side wall is decorated with a carved cross. This is where the pilgrim visiting the sacred city would be reminded that they were now entering holy ground. Touching this cross enabled them to, in modern parlance, 'touch base' with the Lord. The cross-inscribed stone in the wall is also known as the sanctuary stone, because fugitives from justice or those fleeing for other reasons could claim the protection of ecclesiastical sanctuary from the rigours of the law or their enemies once they stood on the holy ground within the gateway. The gateway had at least one upper storey, which served as a lookout point, while oral tradition points to there being a tower above the great archway. On the outside, opposite the gate, lay a paved roadway leading over the mountains and on to the ecclesiastical centres of County Kildare.

Within the sacred city, the most impressive church was the Cathedral of Saints Peter and Paul. Originally named for the Sacred Heart, the cathedral was rededicated to the saints in the twelfth century. Though roofless and ruined, the building is still an imposing one, and evidently went through much refurbishment, remodelling and rebuilding. The chancel is a very fine example of Hiberno-Romanesque architecture. The decoration in this area of the cathedral dates from the ninth and tenth centuries, as does the east window, which was very finely carved, though exposure to the elements has caused much weathering over the centuries. The cathedral was built as a bishop's church, from whence the cleric could speak *ex cathedra* to all in his diocese. Glendalough was a separate diocese in Gaelic Ireland, but after the Normans arrived in Ireland in 1169 they redrew the diocesan boundaries and Glendalough was united with the see of Dublin. This remains the case to this day, and the fact that the Roman Catholic diocese is still referred to as the see of Dublin and Glendalough provides some evidence of the former significance of this isolated and remote Wicklow valley, which is mentioned in ecclesiastical circles in the same breath as Ireland's primate city of well over a million people.

The oldest church in Glendalough is known as the church of Our Lady or St Mary's church, though it may previously have been dedicated to St Ifinus. Measuring approximately 32 feet by 20 feet, it is much smaller than the cathedral, reflecting perhaps the simpler architecture of an earlier stage in the history of the monastic settlement. As the monastery grew its power and influence increased, and when it became a bishopric there was a need for grander buildings. The oldest part of Our Lady's church is the nave, so it was remodelled at least once. A stone altar with an ornamental slab above it, a holy water font and an inscribed cross on the lintel of the west door all bear silent testament to the religious services that once dominated life in this, the monastery's oldest church.

Another feature of interest in the ecclesiastical site is St Kevin's Cross. The high crosses of Celtic Ireland are famed far and wide for their fine stonemasonry. Many, such as the crosses at Monasterboice (County Louth) and Moone (County Kildare), are intricately carved and show scenes from the bible. St Kevin's Cross is different. It is one of the earliest examples of an Irish high cross – it stands about 11 feet 4 inches tall – and one of the plainest. This broad, undecorated, heavy cross made of Wicklow granite traditionally marks the location of St Kevin's grave, though some sources suggest that he was buried in Our Lady's church. Although it is a Celtic cross, with 'arms' around the junction of the vertical and horizontal pieces, St Kevin's Cross is unique in Irish monastic stonemasonry as the arms of the cross are not perforated. It has been suggested that these round arms on Celtic crosses are a throwback to ancient Celtic solar pagan rituals, with the arms representing the sun. However, the circular design may simply have been round buttresses to strengthen the stone crosses, many of which were tall and slim in their execution. According to folklore, anyone who visits Glendalough and who can stand with his or her back to the cross and join hands behind it will have a wish granted to them. As anyone who has ever tried it can testify, this feat is easier said than done!

Possibly the best-preserved building in Glendalough is St Kevin's Kitchen. This church got its nickname from the round belfry, which looks like a chimney, and it is one of the oldest on the site. It dates from *c.* 533 AD and St Kevin supposedly lived here in his later years, after he left his hermitage in the cave known as St Kevin's Bed, high above the waters of the lake. The chancel of the kitchen is no longer extant, but the nave measures approximately 23 feet by 15 feet. The roof is of stone, somewhat similar to earlier corbelled roofs such as that in the passage grave at Newgrange (County Meath), and there may have been an upper floor in the building at one stage. The belfry rises 9 feet above the apex of the roof and contains six small windows, four of which exactly face the cardinal points of the compass. The window in the southern wall of the kitchen was inserted at a later date, in the nineteenth century, when the building was again used for Roman Catholic worship in the post-Penal Laws era, and devotion to St Kevin was once again overtly demonstrated by Irish Catholics in pre-Famine Ireland.

The ruins of the Priests' House are located just south of the cathedral. This was probably the mortuary chapel of the monastic community, and later priests of the local parish were certainly interred here. The building was originally part of the monastery's cemetery, which was much smaller than the present-day graveyard. The Priests' House is not in good repair and many stones are missing, but there is evidence of fine decoration on the east wall and window. In the west wall is the recess of the wishing stone, and the south wall contains an ornamental tympanum, depicting St Kevin between two bishops, one with a crozier and one with a bell. The crozier, or bishop's staff, is a symbol of ecclesiastical authority and the message is clear – Kevin's Glendalough is a bishopric of some significance and an important foundation in the Irish ecclesiastical world. The bell is associated with all monasteries and symbolises the call to prayer. Moreover, one of the most important relics associated with St Patrick is a bell, and the message may aim to show that the authority of Kevin's Glendalough can be traced back to Ireland's patron saint, and that the Irish hierarchy should recognise that Glendalough has great significance as an ecclesiastical site in its own right. The remains of no fewer than five churches – the Cathedral of Saints Peter and Paul, the mortuary chapel of the Priests' House, St Kevin's Kitchen, the church of Our Lady and another church, that of St Ciaran (of which not much is extant), within the monastic city bear ample testament to that significance.

However, no building within the monastic city demonstrates this significance more than the round tower. It is in an excellent state of preservation and the top section, which was struck by lightening, was reconstructed with the original stones in 1876. Round towers are uniquely Irish landmarks, and they were erected in or near many monasteries. Their remains dot the Irish landscape today. Round towers began to feature prominently following the arrival of the Vikings in Ireland. The first Viking attack was on Lambay Island, off the coast of County Dublin, in AD 795. Over the next two centuries or so, the Vikings raided and plundered throughout Ireland, settling down, building towns, intermarrying with local clans and vying for power with those clans until their power was finally broken by the Munster chieftain and Irish high king Brian Boru at the Battle of Clontarf in 1014. Monasteries, with their wealth, were prime targets for Viking raids, and the ever-vigilant monks used round towers as watchtowers. They were also places of safety, and the monks could retreat into them with their treasures, pulling up the ladders behind them as they entered the building through the door inordinately high off the ground. Inside the door a steep stairwell, where the defenders literally had the upper hand, made an uninviting prospect for any attacker who did manage to break through the stout door. These attackers were not always Vikings; the Irish clans suffered much internecine strife and it was not uncommon for clerics such as the Bishop of Glendalough to be dragged into these conflicts. In fact, Glendalough was involved in many such monastic wars over the centuries. When peace reigned over the valley, the round tower also had a more mundane use as a

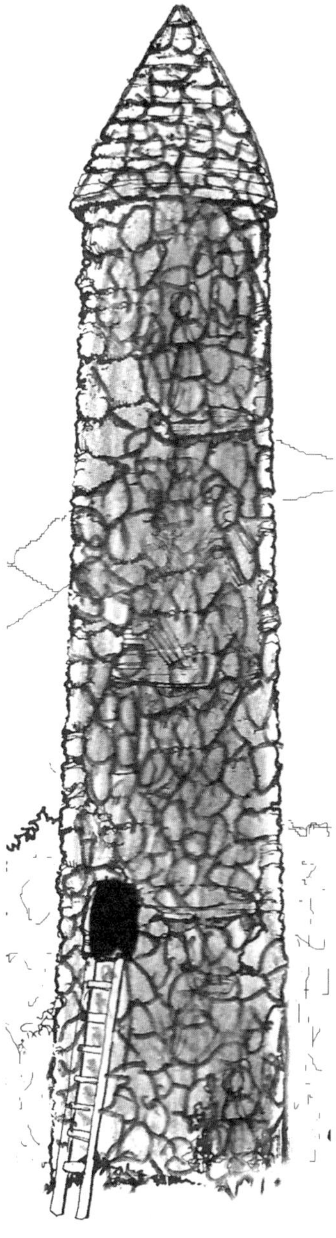

bell tower. The round tower at Glendalough is 103 feet high and has a circumference of over 50 feet at its base, with the only door set high in the wall some 10 feet above ground level. Originally, there were floors at different levels – it seems probable that the building contained seven separate storeys – and four windows precisely matched up with the cardinal points of the compass atop the tower. Glendalough's round tower is the crowing glory of the monastic city, and the top floor must have provided a penthouse with a wonderful view in tranquil times, as well as a safe haven in turbulent times in the valley of the two lakes.

OTHER PLACES OF INTEREST

Across the little Glenealo stream there is a stone containing a small hollow known as the Deer Stone, which is associated with another of St Kevin's miraculous works. Kevin had sympathy for a young widower whose wife had died in childbirth, leaving the man to tend to the newborn infant. Kevin told him to bring the infant to the Deer Stone every day. When Kevin prayed for the man and his infant, a deer arrived daily at the stone and shed her milk into the hollow. The infant survived, thrived and grew up healthy. Local folklore maintains that the hollow in the stone will never dry out, though the continuous moisture in the stone may have more to do with Ireland's maritime climate than with any miraculous occurrence!

Outside the boundaries of the monastic city, the ruins of both Trinity church and the Priory of St Saviour (founded by St Laurence O'Toole in the twelfth century) provide further evidence of the valley's rich ecclesiastical history, bringing the number of churches therein to seven. The old name for Glendalough was Seven Churches, and when a military barracks was built in the area in the early nineteenth century, contemporary documents referred to the location as Seven Churches. This barracks was part of the later history of Glendalough, when the rebel leader Michael Dwyer used the area as a base during his campaign of resistance against the British authorities. Oral tradition maintains that Dwyer used St Kevin's Bed – the cave high over the lake where the saint made his hermitage – as a hideout. A popular story tells of how, from his eyrie-like vantage point, he saw a number of red-coated soldiers searching for him, and when they abandoned their arms for a while on the other side of the lake, the dauntless rebel swam across and captured the muskets, shot and powder, leaving the soldiers to return empty handed after an equally fruitless search for the weapons. One may doubt the accuracy of this particular story, but there is no doubt that Dwyer was involved in many daring escapades from which he emerged unscathed. Perhaps the rebel in Glendalough enjoyed the protection of the saint of Glendalough, who had used the selfsame cave some 1,200 years before!

2

WICKLOW'S GREAT HOUSES

The eighteenth century was an era of building and improvement all across Ireland. The landed elite, who found themselves in possession of most of the land in the country in the wake of the Williamite Wars of the 1680s and 1690s, were in a position of unprecedented power on the island. This encouraged them to accelerate their efforts to shape the landscape in the English model by building country seats and houses, erecting shooting lodges, and founding new villages and improving existing ones. The magnificent scenery of County Wicklow provides a spectacular backdrop to many fine landlord houses. Doubtless the great and the good of the Ascendancy period decided to erect lavish dwellings in keeping both with their own status and with the natural beauty around them. Large country houses were the most obvious symbol of the now universal paternalistic landlord-tenant relationship that concentrated wealth in the hands of the landlords during the eighteenth century. Landlords were linked to their tenants by economic rather than by social ties, and separated from them by language, ethnicity, religion and culture. Landlord mansions, or 'big houses', were home to the landed elite who controlled the country throughout the late seventeenth century.

RATHSALLAGH AND SAUNDERSGROVE

Rathsallagh was one of the earlier houses to be built in the Dunlavin region of west Wicklow. Richard Ryves, who served as Baron of the Irish Exchequer under King William III, retired a wealthy man. In 1703 he commissioned the construction of a new stable at Rathsallagh, so it is likely that the original Rathsallagh house dated from the same period. Ryves's family became influential in County Wicklow. Richard Ryves's eldest son, Thomas, was High Sheriff in 1714, and his son, William, in turn served as High Sheriff in 1734.

The elite became more secure as the eighteenth century advanced and other big houses were constructed throughout County Wicklow. These big houses were the focal points of their surrounding estates, which varied in size from hundreds to thousands of acres. In 1716 Morley Saunders, MP and Second Serjeant-at-Law, purchased an estate near Baltinglass and commissioned Saundersgrove, a large three-storey mansion. Morley Saunders' position as a significant member of the elite was strengthened when he was married, by the Lord Primate of All Ireland, to Martha Stratford of Belan House in County Kildare in 1753. By 1758 Saundersgrove was set on 136 acres of demesne land and was described as follows:

> good for hunting fowling and fishing. The house is fit for any nobleman ... with stabling for above thirty horses ... There are fishponds, a pigeon house and a rabbit-borough, all well stocked. The gardens are in good order, and there is a large orchard, well planted with the choicest kind of apple trees ... and there is a great convenience of water to supply the house and demesne.
>
> (*Universal Advertiser*, 19 December 1758)

The house was completely and elegantly furnished, and the farm stock consisted of the following:

> ewes, wethers and some lambs, a parcel of well-bred horned cattle, two sets of excellent plough cattle, some bay coach horses, draft horses and mares. [Crops included] wheat, barley, oats, beans and vetches.
>
> (*Universal Advertiser*, 26 December 1758)

Saunders was only one of many members of the landed elite in the Wicklow region to construct a fine residence during the eighteenth century. His brother-in-law, George Pendred, who in 1715 succeeded Thomas Ryves as High Sheriff of Wicklow, constructed Fortgranite outside Baltinglass *c.* 1730. Joseph Leeson, the first Earl of Milltown, commissioned the magnificent Russborough House, designed by Richard Cassels (assisted by Francis Bindon) near Blessington, construction of which began in 1741. There are many such examples in the county, from Humewood, the fairy tale castellated residence of the Humes in Kiltegan, to the more modest Avondale House, the seat of the famous Parnell family at Rathdrum. However, two of the most significant and most famous of Wicklow's great houses are situated near Enniskerry and Blessington, respectively: Powerscourt in the east of the county and Russborough in the west.

POWERSCOURT HOUSE AND GARDENS

Although the name might indicate otherwise, Powerscourt was not the country seat of the Power family. The placename actually derives from the reign of Edward I (1272–1307), when a royal castle was located here. The castle was administered by Eustace le Poer, and he implemented the king's laws in the region, holding court here in the medieval period. However, in the middle of the fourteenth century, the O'Toole clan captured the castle and held the lands, with intermittent interruptions, until 1603. That was the year of the Treaty of Mellifont, which ended the Nine Years' War and ushered in the beginning of the end of the Gaelic way of life. Although the O'Tooles petitioned to keep their land, it was actually given to the Wingfield family under the new order. Richard Wingfield, the recipient, was a loyal servant of the Crown, as the grant in the Patent Rolls of James I makes clear:

> Grant to Richard Wingfield, Knt, of the dignity of Viscount Powerscourt in Wicklow County, to hold of him and his heirs male, in consideration of his services in Ireland while a youth, and afterwards as captain in Flanders, as Lt. Col. in France and Portugal under Sir John Norris, and as colonel in the expedition against Cadiz; likewise afterwards under the same general in Ireland, where he received many wounds, and afterwards as Marshal of the Queen's army, under Lord Mountjoy at Kinsale, and on the extinction of Tyrone's rebellion, when O'Dogherty had excited an insurrection in Ulster, having routed him in a pitched battle, and finally having been Lord Justice together with the Archbishop of Dublin, in the absence of Arthur Lord Chichester, Lord Deputy.

There is no trace of the old castle at Powerscourt, but it is probable that it was incorporated into the new Powerscourt House that the Wingfields erected on the site, as parts of the walls were very thick, with window embrasures 8 feet deep, (these were only 2½ feet deep in other parts of the house). And what a house it was. Visitors to Powerscourt cannot but be overwhelmed by its grandeur and its splendid location. The house may have been designed by Richard Cassels, the leading society architect, who was also responsible for many of the finest public buildings in Dublin at this time. Powerscourt House had two fronts: North and South. The North front was decorated with a pediment showing the Wingfield coat of arms on the tympanum; the South front had two circular towers with ogee-shaped copper cupolas at each end. Although there were later additions to the property, notably the terraces, which were begun *c.* 1745 and only finished over a hundred years later in 1867, the house was largely the creation of Richard Wingfield, the first Viscount Powerscourt (this third creation of the title dated from 1743/4), and his second wife Dorothea. The first viscount was a man of substance and he yearned for a house that would reflect his position as a rising star in Irish society even before he received his new title. In 1730 he commissioned the German architect Richard Cassels, who is best-known for transforming Georgian Dublin's city furniture, to design and construct a sixty-eight room mansion, which was finished in 1741. The copper cupolas were reminiscent of a great Italian Renaissance villa and the North front presented a classic Palladian entrance to rival those of similar mansions such as Castletown House in Celbridge and Carton House in Maynooth, both in County Kildare. The South front faced the gardens and a third storey was added in 1787.

Over the years, the influential Wingfield family, the Viscounts Powerscourt, made many improvements and alterations to the interior of the house, while also building up a fine collection of objects d'art throughout their occupancy of Powerscourt. In 1961, however, the ninth viscount sold the house and estate to the Slazenger family, who planned to open the house to the public. They undertook a major refurbishment of the interior, but calamity struck in 1974, when a fire started on the top floor.

The conflagration quickly spread, and the once-magnificent building was reduced to a smouldering shell within a single, fateful night. However, the slow road back was undertaken as repairs began almost immediately, and in 1996 the house was fully re-roofed. The following year, the President of Ireland, Mary Robinson, officially opened the house to the public and a lovingly restored building was available for inspection by a curious clientele, although many of the unique fixtures, furnishings and fittings that had been lost in the fire were irreplaceable. Despite this, Powerscourt House and Gardens was voted into the top ten houses and mansions to visit worldwide by the *Lonely Planet Guide*.

The Lonely Planet's choice is well justified because, as impressive as Powerscourt House was and is, the gardens are still more impressive. Even when the house was closed, the gardens remained open as a major visitor attraction. The location and layout of the gardens is matchless and the superb garden terraces, the deer park and the grounds, including the lofty waterfall (*c.* 400 feet, one of Ireland's highest), mark this as a very special place indeed. It is, without doubt, one of the great showplaces of Europe. Just outside the pretty village of Enniskerry, the entrance to the estate is lined with giant beech trees which were planted over the course of two centuries or so, and the exceptional care taken with that planting has resulted in the trees now being among the foremost attractions of Powerscourt.

Beyond the entrance and in the gardens proper, the terraces command a magnificent vista of the undulating Wicklow landscape, leading to the Great Sugar Loaf Mountain in the background. The gardens borrow the view of the local landscape so well that the Sugar Loaf seems to be part of the vast, ornamental grounds. The upper terrace is 800 feet long and the third terrace is paved with black and white stones in bold geometric patterns, providing a focal point for a vivid design at its centre. The terrace is flanked by eighteenth-century bronze statues, and screened at the sides by wrought iron gates – the wrought ironwork is from the balcony of a castle in Hamburg. As one descends from the terraces, the Triton Pool is immediately ahead. This watery jewel is set amidst a beautiful array of mature trees and contains a fountain which sprays a stream of water more than 60 feet high over the pool. Remarkable statues of the winged horses of Victory and Fame act as silent sentinels beside it.

Powerscourt Gardens contain many subsections. These include the elegant and formal Italian garden; the walled garden with its attractive herbaceous border and ornamental fountains; the Dolphin Pond, where another fountain moves the leaves of water lilies under the shade of eucalyptus trees; the pet cemetery, an unexpected addition where one can read the epitaphs of Powerscourt's pets over the centuries; silent wooded areas and a Japanese garden, where a host of trees and shrubs, some of which are very rare, blend together in perfect Oriental harmony. The whole area of the vast grounds and gardens is a great example of an Ascendancy garden planned with imagination and laid out with excellent taste. As was the case in Heywood, County Laois, the Ascendancy desire to tame the landscape and to establish ownership of it is evident throughout the whole area.

The gardens contain a huge amount of tasteful ironwork, such as the estate's graceful collection of gates. These include the delicate English Gate with its lacelike tracery work nestling between urn-topped columns, the Venetian Gate with its vine-leaf design, and the heavily wrought Bamberg Gate from Bamberg Cathedral with fine craftsmanship in evidence in the intricate scrollwork and ornamental iron flowers. The ironwork of the gates is complemented and offset by a large number of decorative urns and statues, tastefully dispersed throughout the gardens. Another feature is the Pepper Pot Tower, a folly based on the design of an actual pepper pot that was in the possession of the eighth viscount, Mervyn Richard Wingfield. Estate labourers, who used stones from a ruined church in the vicinity, constructed the folly under the direction and watchful eye of the viscount himself. The tower was then decorated with cannon dating back to the time of the Spanish Armada, which threatened England in 1588. The loyalties of the Wingfields were certainly reflected in their garden furniture.

Powerscourt House stood as a symbol of those loyalties, and the superb gardens demonstrated in a tangible way that the Ascendancy had mastered the Irish landscape. The scale, the grandeur, the almost obsessive attention to detail, and the great variety of rare species mark the gardens out as truly significant, and this sense of importance is enhanced by various other delightful aspects of the great estate. The waterfall, reached via a beautiful rhododendron drive, is a prime example, falling, dancing and cascading down an almost sheer rock face, perfectly enhancing the more formal beauty of the gardens and the architectural stature of the house. Today, Powerscourt is one of County Wicklow's major tourist attractions, and it speaks very eloquently of a time when Wicklow and its landscape were owned by an Ascendancy landed elite.

RUSSBOROUGH HOUSE

In the west of County Wicklow too, the frenzy of improvement, the planning of estates, the laying out of demesnes, and the building of great country seats took hold in the eighteenth century. The peace that followed the Williamite Wars lasted for a hundred years or so, and during that time the Ascendancy tried hard to put their own stamp on the Irish landscape. The insecurity of their position as a minority group on an island where the majority were separated from them by language, culture and religion was evident, but they had conquered that majority and now tried to reshape the landscape in a fashion reminiscent of developments in England. The eighteenth century was a boom period for architecture, art, sculpture and decoration in Ireland and the most tangible result of this in west Wicklow was the construction of Russborough House. Two architectural styles of decoration dominated the eighteenth century's big houses. Prior to 1760 or so, the Baroque and Rococo were in vogue, while the later years of the century saw a change as the work of the Adam brothers became fashionable. Russborough, however, falls into the former category, and is one of the best examples of its kind in Ireland.

Russborough was the seat of the Leeson family. Around 1740 when Joseph Leeson, the son of a wealthy Dublin brewer, succeeded to the family fortune – and it was very considerable indeed, as the brewing business was evidently never short of customers – he decided to erect a fine country house to reflect his position as a man of substance, wealth, power and influence. Leeson was also an MP in the Irish parliament in Dublin and from 1743 to 1756 he represented Rathcormack. This coincides almost exactly with the construction of Russborough. Indeed, in 1760 Leeson became Lord Russborough and in 1763 he received the title of Earl of Milltown, as well as being made a member of the Privy Council. By that time, Leeson had a house suitable to his status as the first Earl of Milltown.

Leeson's son succeeded his father as the second earl, and Russborough saw dark days during his tenure. The impact of the rebellion of 1798 was felt all over west Wicklow, and Russborough House was captured and occupied by rebels. Amazingly, no damage was done to the house during this brief occupation, but when the authorities recaptured the house, they decided to station Crown troops there. The soldiers remained billeted in the house for over four years, as west Wicklow remained violent and troubled due to the activities of rebel leader Michael Dwyer, a notorious 'hold-out' who refused to surrender when the main rebellion was crushed. The house suffered a lot of vandalism at the hands of the troops; the interior was damaged, roofs were torn down for firewood, offices and sheds were ruined. The third earl (who had succeeded his bachelor brother) claimed compensation for the damages and losses when the soldiers were finally recalled to barracks, leaving parts of the property as a wrecked empty shell. However, the third earl was in for a shock – all his compensation claims were refused and he was presented with a huge bill for back taxes to cover the period of the military occupation, when the house was out of bounds and uninhabitable by him and his family. The earl cannot have been too pleased!

Nonetheless, the family recovered financially and the house was refurbished during the nineteenth century. The Milltowns remained in possession of the property until 1890, when the sixth earl died. His widow, Geraldine, passed away in 1914 and a nephew, Sir Edmund Turton of Yorkshire, then inherited the house. The Turtons rarely visited Russborough, choosing to remain in England, and the onset of World War One, followed by the Irish War of Independence and the Civil War (collectively known as the Irish 'Troubles' of 1919–23), accentuated the neglect of the house. The decline of Russborough continued until 1931, when Sir Edmund Turton's widow sold it to Captain Denis Daly. The Dalys began the process of rescuing and restoring Russborough, but in 1952 they sold it on to Sir Alfred Beit. Sir Alfred and Lady Beit continued the restoration work and enhanced the fine collection of paintings and objects d'art in the building. In 1972, the house and estate was made over to the Alfred Beit Foundation, a charitable and educational trust that administered the property – now open to the public – on behalf of the Irish state.

The location of Russborough is sublime, and much thought evidently went into the choice of site. Raised on a small embankment, behind the house are a series of artificial terraces, which incorporate a large pond and its island. The house itself is made of Wicklow granite, with the stone coming from the local quarry at Golden Hill. This granite has a very high mica content, which makes it shine and sparkle in the sunlight, especially after a shower of rain. This fairylike quality of the shimmering stone adds to the sense of a special and unusual place.

The entrance and avenue at Russborough are also highly unusual. Most other houses of this importance and scale have long avenues perpendicular to a grand entrance which is often marked out by porches, porticoes and pediments above the doorway. At Russborough though, the visitor enters from the side and a short avenue, lined with mature trees, leads towards what looks like a medium-sized manor house. However, on closer inspection, one may discern roofs and ornamental urns in the background behind this building, and when the visitor proceeds farther along the avenue into the magnificent forecourt, the whole masterly design unfolds in the twinkling of an eye. On the right is the great sweep of the house, with its three sections and two linking colonnades, while on the left the vista suddenly opens up to reveal the extensive grounds, the lake and the Wicklow Mountains forming a glorious backdrop beyond.

Work on building Russborough began *c.* 1741. The German architect Richard Cassels was making a splash among the great and the good of Irish society at this time, and he was the obvious choice for a man such as Joseph Leeson when the design and construction of a fine new country house were on the agenda. Cassels was involved in the ongoing work at

Russborough for a decade; after he died at Carton House in County Kildare in 1751, his associate, Francis Bindon, finished the building of Russborough. The exterior design of the house is Palladian. Andrea Palladio was a famous Venetian architect who modelled much of his work on the classical Roman buildings of ancient Italy. Roman architectural design was described in the writings of the classical author Vitruvius, whose principles of symmetry were clearly outlined in his great work, *De Architectura*. Palladian architecture was certainly symmetrical, and the colonnades emanating from the central block of the main house to the two equidistant wings at Russborough are certainly pleasing to the eye of even the most fastidious and pedantic of symmetry lovers! The stated goal of classical interior design was to reproduce a cubic shape, or to work with variations of the cube. All the ceilings on the ground floor at Russborough were 20 feet high, so there is a sense of similarity and continuity as the visitor moves from room to room. The classical lines and proportions conform very well to the Palladian ideal.

Palladio was a Renaissance figure, but the Palladian mansion at Russborough was an eighteenth-century project, so the interiors of the house would be unrecognisable to Palladio, the interior of whose own works in Italy were decorated simply in the Renaissance style. However, Baroque and Rococo interiors were in vogue when Russborough was built, and a superfluity of overflowing plasterwork is in evidence everywhere in the house. Walls, ceilings and staircase all exude light and elegant stucco work.

Much of the stucco work at Russborough was executed by the Francini brothers, Philip and Paul. These Italian master craftsmen were busily employed on many great projects in Ireland at this time, and were the crème de la crème of interior designers to the Irish Ascendancy. Their stucco ceilings at Russborough are among the best examples of their art. The ceiling of the saloon with its cherubs, flowers, plants and ornamental extras is hugely playful and exudes the confidence and ebullience of this Golden Age of Anglo-Irish architecture. The drawing room also has stucco work on its walls, with oval decorations forming a housing for four similarly shaped paintings by Joseph Vernet.

There are many other architectural delights at Russborough, but the collection of fine art in the house is also highly significant. Alfred Beit made his fortune in the diamond mines of South Africa. He was a co-founder of the De Beers Consolidated Mines diamond mining company and, as his wealth increased, he began to collect fine art, principally Renaissance paintings and sculptures. Guided by Dr Wilhelm Bode, director of the Kaiser Friedrich Museum in Berlin, Beit later turned his attention to Dutch, Flemish and Spanish art, which came to dominate the Beit collection by the time it was moved to Russborough. Much of the collection may still be viewed in situ in the house, although some of the most valuable pieces have been moved following a series of robberies.

Sir Alfred Beit actually purchased Russborough to act as a repository for his wonderful collection of art. However, there have been four separate art thefts at the house. In 1974 the IRA stole twelve paintings from Russborough. Rose Dugdale, a hard-line Republican, masterminded the operation. The theft was intended to raise money for the Republican cause and would also help to spring Dugdale's boyfriend from prison! However, stealing famous works of art proved easier than finding a market for them, and all twelve paintings were found in County Cork. In 1986, a well-known Dublin gangland criminal, Martin Cahill, also known as 'The General', executed another daring raid on Russborough's art collection. Cahill and his men stole eighteen paintings, but again selling them on proved difficult. Bit by bit the hoard was recovered and sixteen of the eighteen paintings are now back in the collection. Some of these pictures were recovered in 'sting' operations and, in addition to the British Isles, were located in places as far away as Turkey and the Netherlands. Cahill was later the victim of a gangland-style execution in Dublin. Smaller robberies were carried out in both

2001 and 2002, but all of the paintings stolen in these thefts have been recovered. The robberies persuaded the custodians of Russborough House to move the most valuable paintings, including works by Jan Vermeer, Thomas Gainsborough and Francisco Goya. These are now housed in the National Gallery of Ireland in Dublin, where a wing of the building now bears the Beit name as a demonstration of gratitude for the donation of these priceless paintings. Despite the loss of these works of art, there is still a fine collection of paintings at Russborough, and the architectural detail, the interior furnishings and fittings including silver, porcelain, tapestries, furniture and carpets, and the extensive grounds all make it an excellent place to visit, so it remains among the top historical attractions in County Wicklow.

3

WICKLOW REBELS

The wild and mountainous landscape of County Wicklow meant that it harboured more than its fair share of rebels over the centuries. Two of the best known were Feagh Mac Hugh O'Byrne from Glenmalure and Michael Dwyer from the Glen of Imaal.

FEAGH MAC HUGH O'BYRNE: 'THE FIREBRAND OF THE WICKLOW MOUNTAINS'

> Lift Mac Cahir Óg your face; brooding o'er the old disgrace,
> that black Fitzwilliam stormed your place and drove you to the Fern.
> Grey said victory was sure; soon the firebrand he'd secure,
> Until he met at Glenmalure, Feagh Mac Hugh O'Byrne.
>
> (P.J. McCall, *Follow Me Up to Carlow*, 1899)

For many people, the name Feagh Mac Hugh O'Byrne is synonymous with County Wicklow, and they refer to him as one of the first leaders in that county to oppose British rule. The rise of the O'Byrne clan (and particularly the Gabhal Raghnaill sept) during the long sixteenth century facilitated the resistance of Feagh and some of his forebears to the Crown. Feagh made a significant contribution to Irish affairs in the sixteenth century, especially during both the Baltinglass rebellion and the Nine Years' War. The latter was primarily a revolt by Ulster chieftains under Hugh O'Neill, the Earl of Tyrone, but there was also a Wicklow focus of unrest, where Feagh Mac Hugh's resilience and tenacity in the face of adversity demonstrated why he earned the sobriquet 'the firebrand of the Wicklow Mountains'.

By Feagh's final year (1597), Lord Deputy Russell had identified him as 'the cheife rebel of Lynster', indicating the progress made by the Gabhal Raghnaill sept of the O'Byrne clan as the sixteenth century progressed. During the early part of that century, Leinster was governed by the Kildares. Garret Mór FitzGerald, eighth Earl of Kildare, ruled with an iron fist, especially after his victory over the rebellious Burke and his allies at Knockdoe on 19 August 1504. The influence of the Kildares spread and in 1508 the 'Duties upon Irishmen' in their rental listing of Gaelic Irish leaders from whom they received tributes included all the major chiefs of Leinster, with the O'Byrnes prominent among them. However, Garret Mór died in September 1513, and his successor, Garret Óg, did not wield the same control. He suffered some embarrassing defeats at the hands of the native Irish, and the success of the O'Byrnes' raid on Dublin Castle in 1533 underlined both the decline of the earls of Kildare and the advancement of the Wicklow clan. In 1534, the two factions actually joined forces during the revolt of Silken Thomas, the Earl of Kildare, but this was ultimately crushed and Thaddeus, the chief of the O'Byrnes, submitted to Henry VIII in 1535. In 1536 he promised to be a faithful subject, not to maintain rebels, and to pay monies to the king in return for possession of his lands and the protection of the lord deputy. However, the Henrician Reformation represented a seachange in political as well as religious relationships in Ireland, and aspects of the Kildare revolt indicated that there were many Irishmen (and Anglo-Normans) whose Catholicism could be invoked to undermine loyalties to the English monarchy.

The mid-sixteenth century witnessed a game of cat and mouse regarding such loyalties, played out between the English authorities and the Gaelic chiefs. At one stage, Thaddeus O'Byrne even requested that his territory be shired. As Sir John Davies recalled, 'the Byrnes of the mountains, in the thirty-fourth year of Henry VIII [1542] desired that their county might be made shire ground and called the county of Wicklow'. However the clan rejected this proposal, removed Thaddeus from the leadership and elected a new chief, Shane Mac Redmond, who opposed this scheme. This period witnessed continuing sporadic clashes between the O'Byrnes and the authorities. In 1548 for example, Shane's son, Hugh Mac Shane O'Byrne, threatened the Boystown area, occupying it with sixty kernes for three days. In 1566, Hugh Mac Shane raided Ballymore Eustace, which lay on the very boundary of the Pale (the area in the east of the country controlled by England), and exacted black rents there. These actions pointed to Hugh's belligerent intentions, and increased the rising power of the Gabhal Raghnaill sept, which emerged as the leading branch of the O'Byrne clan during this time. Hugh's Gabhal Raghnaill was a formidable force, and they regularly embarked on raids and expeditions against contiguous English settlements. Edmund Spenser's *View of the State of Ireland* confirmed the improved fortunes of the clan under Hugh's leadership.

It was Hugh's son, Feagh, however, who truly figured among the foremost Gaelic leaders of his age. He was born around 1544. As a young man, Feagh was involved in Sir Edmund Butler's escape from Dublin Castle in 1569, and was implicated in the murder of Robert Browne in Wexford in 1572. Crucially, he grew to maturity at a time when his

clan's fortunes were waxing. However, Elizabeth I was crowned in 1558, and her administration sought to impose strict control over Ireland. Such a policy was opposed to the Gaelic way of life and the social control wielded by the O'Byrnes and other clans. The stage was thus set for further conflict.

Feagh proved to be a thorn in the side of the Dublin administration throughout the 1560s and 1570s. In 1563, Feagh and his father captured two captains, Henry Davells and George Harvey, probably with the intention of holding them for ransom. The prisoners were eventually released and the abductors pardoned, but Feagh's lengthy campaign of resistance had begun. Kinship bonds and close family loyalties were a significant feature of Gaelic Ireland, and in 1572 Feagh joined his brother-in-law, Rory Óg O'More of Laois, to attack the Pale. Later in that decade, on 21 September 1578, Feagh submitted to Lord Justice Drury at Christ Church Cathedral. The game of cat and mouse with the authorities continued; in all Feagh was pardoned seven times for treachery against the Crown. By the beginning of 1580, Rory Óg had been killed (but not before he had burned Naas in retaliation for the massacre of Mullaghmast in 1577) and Feagh and his followers had been pacific for a little over a year. This situation changed dramatically with the outbreak of the Desmond rebellion in Munster, an event that received papal support. In Wicklow, Feagh supported the rebellion of Viscount Baltinglass, with this support culminating in the heavy defeat of English forces at Glenmalure on 25 August 1580. Baltinglass was a religious zealot, tackling Gaelic grievances in the name of Catholicism, but Feagh seems not to have shared his convictions. However, Catholicism had been invoked once again, and Feagh rallied to the cause. Although he did not fully share the fundamentalist Catholic zeal of the viscount, he was not unaware of the Counter-Reformation ideas spreading to Ireland at the time, and ensured that the papal standards were raised in Leinster during the insurrection, hoisting the papal banner over the still smouldering castle of Newcastle McKynegan in 1580. Feagh was at the height of his power, and his crushing victory over Lord Arthur Grey de Wilton at Glenmalure marked the zenith of his military achievements.

Defeat at Glenmalure was a huge setback for the authorities. The event had all the hallmarks of a total rout, and casualties were very high: the *Annals of Loch Cé* estimated the number of English casualties at 909. Glenmalure was one of the heaviest defeats ever suffered by Crown forces in Ireland. It caused panic within the Pale and on the streets of the capital, where a follow-up attack by Feagh's forces was expected almost hourly once the calamitous news had come through. Feagh, however, did not possess the military strength for such a risky undertaking, so he remained in the mountains awaiting developments. Victory was sweet but short-lived.

The rebellion ultimately failed, but highland Wicklow was still firmly in O'Byrne's possession. It is true that Sir William Stanley burnt Feagh's settlement at Ballinacor in April 1581, but its remote nature made it difficult to hold and Feagh and his followers soon reoccupied the area. Throughout most of the 1580s and 1590s, the highland Wicklow region was referred to as 'O'Byrnes' Country' or 'Feagh Mac Hugh's Country', and the chief's presence so close to Dublin was both an embarrassment and a challenge to the authorities. The suitability of the Ballinacor site for defence meant that the O'Byrnes had no need to construct a stone fortification, and a wooden fort was deemed sufficient for their needs. From Glenmalure, the clan had access to Glendalough and the Glen of Imaal, providing routes towards both the Pale and lowland Leinster, with an emergency escape path via the plateau atop Table Mountain to the northwest.

The 1590s witnessed an escalation of hostilities. Red Hugh O'Donnell and Art O'Neill escaped from Dublin Castle in 1591. They headed towards Glenmalure. After great hardship, which caused the death of O'Neill in the Wicklow Mountains, O'Donnell reached O'Byrnes' country. There is no documentary evidence to support the premise that local mountain dwellers aided the escape, as any loyalties owed by Wicklow peasants to a prince from Donegal were, at the very least, probably quite tentative. Nonetheless, the event created a bond of sorts between Feagh and Red Hugh, possibly strengthened by a sense of Gaelic identity and by Counter-Reformation Catholicism.

In May 1593 Red Hugh O'Donnell, with the help of Archbishop Magauran, organised a confederation; later that year, Hugh Maguire began his military campaign. O'Donnell joined him in 1594 and, crucially, O'Neill did likewise in 1595. Also in that year, Feagh was declared a traitor and a large reward was offered for his capture or his head. In 1596 Feagh formally allied himself with Hugh O'Neill, and took the field on 9 September, gambling on a successful Spanish landing. However, the shipwreck of the 'second armada' off Coruna on 13 October sealed Feagh's fate. Following news of the ships' destruction, Lord Deputy Sir William Russell returned to Wicklow to put Feagh and his army to flight. The old chief was discovered in a cave in Glenmalure and killed by a Sergeant Milburne (under the command of Captain Thomas Lee) on 7 May 1597. Feagh was decapitated and his head was placed on a spike over the entrance to Dublin Castle. Despite this, hostilities continued briefly under the leadership of Feagh's son and successor Phelim Mac Feagh O'Byrne, but by the dawn of the new century this revolt was also crushed and the Wicklow region was at last ripe for plantation.

From the late 1570s onwards, Feagh Mac Hugh O'Byrne was the foremost Gaelic chief in Leinster, ably succeeding his brother-in-law Rory Óg Ó More in that role after the latter's death. Feagh's participation in the Baltinglass revolt, and his resounding victory at Glenmalure in 1580, raised his profile considerably and catapulted him to national prominence. Feagh's use of Gaelic identity, his adherence to Catholicism, his record on the field of battle, his complex relationships with other Gaelic chiefs and with Baltinglass all point to diplomatic adroitness, military skill, political adaptability and a keen instinct for survival. Feagh's involvement in the Nine Years' War and the longevity of his military operations in highland

Wicklow drained the resources of the Crown forces, which needed to maintain a constant military presence to protect areas of adjacent lowland Leinster and the Pale from attack. Feagh's death was a severe blow to O'Neill's cause, and in 1598, when the earl was most in need of the O'Byrnes to keep the forces of the Pale occupied, it deprived the great earl of support and the use of highland Wicklow as a diversionary theatre. In the final analysis, Feagh's military operations were a distraction within a larger conflict, and his standing was not on a par with that of Tyrone, but as the earl's powerful Leinster ally, his support aided the rise of Hugh O'Neill and his attempt to defeat English forces – an attempt which almost succeeded.

MICHAEL DWYER: 'THE WICKLOW CHIEF'

Have you heard of Michael Dwyer and his mountain men?
Runs your blood like molten fire when you hear again
How he dashed like mountain torrent on his country's bitter foes
Like a thundering, tearing torrent on the craven yeos?

(Peadar Kearney, *Michael Dwyer and his Mountain Men*)

Michael Dwyer was born in the Glen of Imaal in 1772, the son of a small tenant farmer, and he grew up among the people of this glen. Making a living, especially from farming, was difficult in this remote region deep in the Wicklow Mountains. The Dwyers were not rich – Michael's parents, John and Mary, were ordinary people. The Dwyers were Roman Catholic, so Michael was educated at a hedge school by Peter Burr, a remarkable figure. He was a graduate of the strictly Protestant Trinity College, Dublin, but he was also a progressive thinker, who kept up with political changes brought about by the American and French revolutions. Burr made sure that Michael Dwyer and his other pupils also knew about these changes.

The establishment of the United Irishmen in Belfast in 1791 fuelled Loyalist fears in Ireland. In the Glen of Imaal, Peter

Burr was among the first to join the new organisation of United Irishmen. Burr's action probably influenced his old pupil, who became even more politically aware as new ideas infiltrated the Glen. In 1797, Michael Dwyer also joined the Society of United Irishmen, which had been banned in 1793, and became a wanted man.

While Dwyer was evading the authorities, the 1798 rebellion broke out in west Wicklow (and Kildare). On the opening day of the uprising, there was a horrendous massacre of political prisoners who had been incarcerated in the local market house in Dunlavin. The effects of this event were far reaching. News of the slaughter was one of the factors that prompted Fr John Murphy to rebel in Wexford. Dwyer went to Wexford, where he joined the rebels. (At this stage, Dwyer was a captain in the United Irishmen.) The North Wexford campaign eventually led the rebels across the border into Wicklow and to the town of Arklow, which was the scene of the next battle. Dwyer's bravery was noted at the Battle of Arklow, but despite his courage and that of others, the Battle of Arklow was a major defeat for the rebels, who had to retreat back to Wexford.

Following an action at Kilcavan Hill, Dwyer and his comrades reached Vinegar Hill on 20 June. This was the eve of what was be the decisive government victory of the campaign in the south-east. Vinegar Hill was another major defeat for the insurgents, and marked the beginning of the end of the rising. On 21 June, the rebel forces broke and the main body retreated southwards towards Wexford town. Dwyer, however, retreated northwards, rejoining some of his comrades on the way. They spent that night at Peppard's Castle and reached the sacked settlement of Aughrim on 24 June. The survivors of Vinegar Hill began to regroup. Their commander, Garret Byrne of Ballymanus, now decided to attack Hacketstown, just over the county border in Carlow on 25 June.

At Hacketstown Michael Dwyer was given his first significant command as he led one of the rebel flanking parties. However, determined Loyalist defence meant that the attackers' losses were high as the defenders picked them off from within stone buildings. Solid resistance from well-armed forces within well-fortified positions amply demonstrated that, without cannon, the rebels could not hope to take such positions. Once again, Dwyer's courage was noted at Hacketstown. With two brothers named Laffan from Kilmuckridge, he managed to climb the barracks wall using scaling ladders. Despite this gallant effort, the barracks proved too tough a nut to crack and the rebels eventually had to withdraw.

The tide of war had firmly turned in favour of the government forces. Retreat into the fastnesses of the Wicklow Mountains was now the only sensible option for the beleaguered rebel forces, but Michael Dwyer could scarcely have imagined just how long his resistance would last in these remote valleys as he and his comrades trekked towards Glenmalure in the first week of July 1798. For a while, Dwyer defended the secluded glen and at this time was referred to as 'the Governor of Glenmalure'. However, Michael Dwyer evacuated Glenmalure with the remainder of the insurgents on 6 August and arrived in the Glen of Imaal the next day. He was home! The Glen of Imaal was geographically remote and the community within it was a close-knit one, which meant that Dwyer had many friends ready to shelter him.

Dwyer and his men decided to continue the fight and September saw him involved in the Battle of Keadeen. This was the first in a series of indecisive skirmishes in which the rebels harried and harassed the Crown forces. Dwyer, who realised that pitched battles had been disastrous, was probably the first Irish rebel leader to employ such 'hit and run tactics' and Michael Collins cited Dwyer as an inspiration for his own guerrilla campaigns during the War of Independence over 120 years later. Such a campaign suited Dwyer, who was on home territory and who was a fieldcraft expert with finely-honed survival skills.

Dwyer's guerrilla campaign continued into 1799. There is no doubt that many of Michael Dwyer's exploits were hair-raising – the real stuff of which ballads were made. Narrow escapes such as the evasion of detection by assuming the disguise of a beggar man and boldly passing by the soldiers who were seeking him or lying across the rafters of Mangan's house while the yeomen searched the building at ground level rank right up there with the legendary Robin Hood! Dwyer's most famous exploit during his guerrilla campaign was probably also his narrowest escape. This occurred at the cottage of Miley Connell in Derrynamuck on the night of 15 February 1799. For once, Dwyer's lookout system had failed to alert him of approaching danger. Information received from a spy had led the military to the very door of Dwyer's refuge. Connell's cottage was the third in a *clachan* of three, situated at the end of an isolated boreen. The rebel occupants of the other two cottages had already been taken. Ned Lennon and Thomas Clerk surrendered at Hoxey's house and Wat McDonnell (McDaniel), Patrick Toole, John Ashe, John Mickle, Hugh Byrne and Darby Dunn were captured at the home of the Toole family. The military, a detachment of Scottish Highlanders led by Captain Roderick McDonald, surrounded Connell's cottage and called on the men inside – Michael Dwyer, Sam McAllister, Patrick Costello and John Savage – to surrender. They refused and Costello and Savage were killed in the ensuing battle of Derrynamuck. Sam McAllister also lost his life, which he sacrificed in order to give Dwyer himself a chance to escape. Dwyer emerged from the cottage and, barefoot and in his underclothes, burst through the Scottish line and ran to freedom. Dwyer was the only member of the rebel band to escape that night. The others were all either killed or captured.

Dwyer's mountain campaign of guerrilla warfare would continue long after his escape from Derrynamuck in February 1799. Dwyer was involved in many dangerous escapades, near misses and scary moments, which became the subject of many ballads, ensuring the stories of his exploits were ingrained in popular culture. Dwyer's legend had been growing throughout his guerrilla campaign and posthumous literary works would later elevate him to hero status. His prolonged resistance in the Wicklow Mountains had touched a communal nerve. Dwyer was more than an outlaw, more than a rebel, and more than a guerrilla leader to many people. He was a symbol of hope at a time and in a place of oppression. As long as there was any hope, however slight, of another revolution or another French invasion, Dwyer would remain in his mountain lair and await developments.

However, as the years passed, hope of such developments faded. By 1803, the Treaty of Amiens of the previous year, although short-lived, had shattered any remaining hope of French intervention in Ireland. In July of that year, Robert Emmet's attempted revolution had petered out. Meanwhile, the net was tightening on Dwyer and his followers. The completion of the Military Road from Dublin through the mountains was a major boost for the Crown forces. Military barracks were occupied at strategic points along the road. This considerably hindered Dwyer's capacity for movement in the heart of the mountains. In addition, the military had unleashed a campaign of arrests against known or suspected friends and relations of Dwyer. This strained Dwyer's kinship network almost to breaking point. The situation was very bleak for the remnants of Dwyer's pitifully small force as the winter of 1803 drew in. Michael Dwyer's thoughts turned to ending his guerrilla campaign and the drawing up of terms that would allow him to lay down his arms.

Dwyer made overtures to the MP, William Hume of Humewood. General Beresford wanted Dwyer to surrender upon the mercy of government (i.e unconditionally), but Hume gave some assurances to Mary Dwyer, his wife. Certainly Dwyer's life was to be spared, and safe passage to America was possibly agreed upon. Dwyer may have been led to believe that he would obtain a full pardon on surrendering himself. Whatever the truth of the situation, there is no doubt that the United Irish Captain Michael Dwyer laid down his arms on what he believed were his own terms when he walked though the gates of Humewood and into the custody of William Hoare Hume on 14 December 1803, thus bringing to an end the brilliant guerrilla campaign which had elevated him to the status of myth.

However, once the authorities had their man, they did not adhere to the terms that had been outlined. Michael Dwyer remained a prisoner in Kilmainham jail from December 1803 to August 1805, as did some of his men. Eventually Dwyer's fate was decided upon and Dwyer found out that he was bound for the penal colony of Australia. Michael Dwyer's captivity in Ireland ended in August 1805, when, in company with his wife Mary and some of his rebel comrades, the leader from the Glen of Imaal boarded the *Tellicherry* at Queenstown (now Cobh), bound for Botany Bay.

On arrival in Australia in 1806, the Wicklow rebels were each given 100 acres of land at Cabramatta. However, Governor William Bligh was paranoid about the possibility of an uprising in the colony and, in view of their background, he saw the Wicklow settlers as a huge threat. Dwyer was arrested as a possible ringleader of a rebellion that had not taken place and kept in solitary confinement on board the HMS *Porpoise*. Following an elaborate show trial, Dwyer was found guilty of 'conspiracy in order to raise a rebellion' and in May 1807 was sent to the convict depot on Norfolk Island.

Dwyer was moved from Norfolk Island to Van Dieman's Land in January 1808. With the departure of Bligh, however, Michael Dwyer and his companions were pardoned and released from captivity. Under the more enlightened Governor Lachlan Macquarie, Dwyer was appointed a constable at George's River on 25 August 1810. By 1819 Dwyer owned 620 acres and the solid expansion of his land holding was further proof of his acumen and ability. In May 1820, Dwyer was appointed Chief Constable of Liverpool in New South Wales.

However, Dwyer had also invested in a tavern called the Harrow Inn. This was perhaps not a good move on the part of a man who was well known to have a fondness for alcohol. The public house brought financial problems and Dwyer was removed from his position as chief constable due to misconduct. To boost his finances, Dwyer had illegally charged rent for land belonging to a woman named Ann Stroud. On Christmas Eve 1822, he was found guilty of 'having broken the colonial regulations' and was fined £20. More seriously, however, he lost his spirit licence and was unable to pay his creditors. In 1824 he was incarcerated in the debtors' prison in Sydney. He was released in May 1825, but was in poor health when he returned to one of his few possessions that had not been sold – his house at Cabramatta. Weak and suffering from dysentery, Michael Dwyer died on 23 August 1825.

However, the death of Michael Dwyer in Australia only strengthened the legend of the wronged leader who was shamefully exiled by a deceitful establishment. Dwyer had been so well known during his guerrilla campaign that he had captured the public imagination, and he remains to this day an icon of Irish resistance to the authorities.

4

CRIME AND PUNISHMENT: TALES FROM WICKLOW'S DARK SIDE

A HANGING IN HOLLYWOOD

In 1641 a rebellion erupted in Ireland. The event can be seen in the context of a wider religious conflict raging throughout Europe, and the Irish rebels were predominantly Catholic while their opponents were mainly Protestant. The violence quickly took on a sectarian nature. The rebellion went on from 1641 to 1653 and there is copious evidence to suggest that unrest was widespread throughout all of County Wicklow during this period. The 1641 depositions (Loyalist claims for compensation after the rebellion) paint a picture of turmoil in nearly every village and parish. For example, Henry Harrington of Grangecon claimed that a band of rebels that included Thomas Moore, John Lawler and Marcus Graham caused huge destruction. Harrington's claim listed (among other things) livestock including 'five hundred and seventeen sheep of English breed' valued at £115, bedding and household goods worth £50 and the destruction of haggards and barns worth

£400, and he claimed £1,500 because he lost his 'interest in lands at Grangecon and Griffinstowne' which belonged to his father. Harrington's total claim reached the huge total of £2,535 10*s*, making it among the most sizeable in Wicklow. All the deponents refer to raids on property perpetrated by rebels and provide evidence of the extent of the violence, the damage to agriculture, the large-scale economic disruption and the huge impact of the rebellion throughout Wicklow. The total damage estimated by the 65 loyal subjects examined in the county was £132,457 14*s* 2*d*. Only counties Cavan, Monaghan and Fermanagh recorded higher totals nationally.

It is evident from the depositions that the rebels raided and plundered throughout west Wicklow with impunity during the rebellion. However, the depositions also reveal deeper underlying issues dividing settler and native in the region, and violence as a manifestation of deep-seated religious and socio-economic grievances. The best-documented example relates to the hanging of a Protestant woman named Jane Fflood (Flood) in Hollywood during the spring of 1642.

Jane, the wife of Philip Flood of Naas, was in Hollywood when rebels under the command of Anthony and Donal Oge McDonnell attacked the village. The rebels found her and were fearful that she might inform on them to the authorities if she were allowed to return to Naas. She was given no chance to defend herself as no trial was held, but rough justice was meted out in the form of summary execution. Some of the 'said robbers took away the said Jane Flood and carried her out of the town to a wood about two miles away... and [she] was hanged by the said rebels'. William Mandefield witnessed the incident and deposed that a certain John Murfy was the ringleader of the rebels responsible for the hanging. According to Nicholas Buckley, Morgan Donnell of Hollywood accompanied Murfy, also of Hollywood, and they hanged Jane Flood. Her body was left uninterred, but Buckley also stated that a lady named Sarah, whose surname he did not know, brought a winding sheet and helped to bury Jane Flood three days later.

Both Murfy and Morgan McDonnell (the Morgan Donnell referred to by Buckley) gave evidence before the commission in March 1653. McDonnell denied knowing either Jane Flood or her husband Philip, while Murfy admitted knowing them, but denied complicity in the murder, stating however that he had heard that the Irish rebels had hanged her. McDonnell's deposition was given through an interpreter. At least one other deposition regarding the case was also given thus, suggesting that Irish was the language of the native residents of west Wicklow at this time. The verdict handed down to Murfy and McDonnell was not recorded in the depositions, but it is likely that they were found guilty. Murfy's father Phelim, also a rebel, was certainly dead by October 1653. The summary execution of Jane Flood points to the existence of sharp ethnic animosities in the county. Jane Flood, a Protestant, was in the wrong place at the wrong time. Her execution by the rebels may have been a strategic military decision, but the rebels only perceived it to be so because of her Protestantism. In this context, the episode also becomes a manifestation of sectarianism, and attests to an undercurrent of sectarianism in the region during the mid-seventeenth century. Time and again this sectarian undercurrent surfaced in County Wicklow, sometimes manifesting itself with frightening ferocity. Sectarianism often arises when one group (in this case the Catholic majority) harbour constant resentment for real and perceived wrongs, while another group (in this case the Protestant minority) live in constant fear of real or imagined reprisals and violence. For Jane Flood in 1642, this led to 'lynch law' being implemented in Hollywood.

A BLUDGEONING IN BARNDARRIG

A murder in the sleepy village of Barndarrig in east Wicklow in 1890 led to the last hanging in Wexford gaol in 1892. Barndarrig lies between Wicklow town and Arklow and it was a quiet backwater in the late nineteenth century. The area had witnessed no significant trouble since the Great Famine of the 1840s when it came to national prominence because of the murder of an elderly lady named Mary Ann Lyons. Mrs Lyons was 65 years of age and well known in the village, as she kept a local shop. She also lived on the premises; her living quarters were adjacent to the little shop, both being under the same cottage roof. Locally it was rumoured that she had a huge fortune stashed away in the house and there was speculation that this was the reason that she preferred not to serve customers after dark. However, village life being what it was, many people ignored her preferences and customers often knocked on her doors after hours to purchase some daily necessity. Mary Ann had some money saved, though not the miser's hoard that many people believed. However, the cunning old dame gave most of it to her friend – the local schoolteacher – for safekeeping, keeping a smaller amount for herself in case of emergency transactions. She hid this money in the clock in her sitting room.

One Sunday evening in December 1890, a Barndarrig villager named James Kehoe visited his neighbours, the Handleys. These two brothers, Daniel in his twenties and the teenaged James, were well known characters in the village and were slightly late arriving for their meeting with Kehoe. The brothers were known to be poachers, but had no serious criminal convictions to their names. The men spent a pleasant evening chatting and relaxing. Kehoe probably told the brothers that he had been to Lyons' shop to buy tobacco earlier in the evening. He saw a light on inside and had knocked on the door, but the light was immediately extinguished and he received no answer, so he left empty handed, assuming the old lady did not want to serve him for some reason.

Mary Ann Lyons, however, had not refused to serve her customer. The next day the schoolteacher found her friend's body in a pool of blood on the floor of her cottage bedroom. The whole place had been ransacked, and it seemed probable that the robbers had killed the old woman with a vicious blow to the head, perhaps to stop her from identifying them. Such murders were rare in Ireland at the time, and rarer still in sleepy

Barndarrig. The police set to work and brought in six men who had been seen on the street in the village the previous night for questioning. These included James Kehoe and both Daniel and James Handley. Kehoe told the police about his unanswered visit to the shop and also mentioned the late arrival of the Handleys. When asked if he noticed anything unusual about the brothers at the time, Kehoe claimed that they both looked like they had had a bit of a shock. He went on to say that James's clothes were wet, which was strange as it hadn't been raining, and that Daniel had some blood on his mouth. Daniel had explained that he had caught himself on a thorny bush.

A cut mouth and wet clothes on known poachers hardly constituted proof of murder, and when the Handleys were questioned they suggested that James Keogh could quite easily have killed the old lady himself. However, in a search of the Handley home the police found a large wad of tobacco, 17½ ounces in weight, which was the same type as the tobacco sold by Mary Ann Lyons in her shop. Again the evidence was hardly overwhelming, but the police also found a halfpenny coin which had a hole drilled in the image of Queen Victoria's head. People remembered that the coin had been in the shop, but Daniel Handley claimed that Mrs Lyons gave it to him in his change the last time he was in the shop and it would be difficult, if not impossible to prove otherwise! There was not much to go on, but in spite of the flimsy nature of the available evidence, the Handley brothers were both arrested and charged with the murder of Mary Ann Lyons.

It was decided that the brothers should be tried separately. The trials would be complicated, however, due to the lack of hard evidence and the fact that Irish juries were notoriously difficult to convince when it came to capital charges such as murder. Daniel Handley was tried twice, in both Wicklow and Carlow, but twice the juries could not agree on a verdict. This prompted the authorities to delay the trial of James Handley for the same offence, which meant that both men were tried together for the murder in Wicklow in March 1892.

It was James's first trial and Daniel's third. This time though, there was a significant difference – this would be a trial by special jury. In essence, this was a legal device whereby the jury was handpicked, and usually nationalist supporters of any kind were excluded from these juries. Although the crime was not a political one, the accused men came from a lower class nationalist background, and a special jury was unlikely to have any sympathy for them. On 19 March 1892, Daniel Handley was found guilty of the murder of Mrs Mary Ann Lyons. When the verdict was announced, Daniel shouted out, 'I ain't guilty'. When asked whether he had anything to say before the death sentence was pronounced, Daniel made the telling and suggestive remark, 'I didn't strike the final blow'. Considering this revelation, it was a strange twist when the jury also found James guilty of the crime but recommended clemency for him because of his young age and due to the fact that he was operating under the influence of his elder brother.

The verdicts had been given, but many people in Wicklow did not agree with them. The lack of evidence was glaring, and many thought that the Handleys were actually innocent of the crime. However, the law inexorably took its course, and it was announced that both brothers would be executed in Wexford gaol. A campaign for a reprieve began. The mayor of Wicklow instigated a protest in the town council. Irish MPs referred to the case when they asked questions in the House of Commons in London. Popular protests were organised throughout Ireland using the slogan 'You can't hang a Wicklow man in Wexford'. All the efforts were in vain. The authorities refused to change the sentence or the venue. However, in light of the special jury's recommendation, James Handley's sentence was commuted to 15 years' penal servitude. About a hundred people gathered at the gate of Wexford gaol on the morning of 19 April 1892. Inside, the English hangman, Thomas Scott, did his duty when Daniel Handley walked alone to the gallows which had been constructed in a shed beside the prison hospital. Daniel began to shake and had to be restrained by prison officers. He said 'Goodbye

Father' to the priest in attendance, who replied 'Goodbye Dan'. The prison bell pealed at 7.45 am, and the crowd outside the gate knew that the murder of Mary Ann Lyons had been avenged – although not many believed that the right man had paid the price.

In a final bizarre twist, although Daniel Handley was the last man to be hanged in Wexford gaol, his was not the last execution in the prison. The gaol closed in 1903 and became a home for alcoholics, but during the Irish Civil War of 1922–23, the national army of the Irish Free State used it as a military base. This was the political backdrop when, on 13 March 1923, three Irregulars (anti-treaty IRA men) – John Crean aged 19, Patrick Hogan aged 19 and James Parle aged 25 – were executed by firing squad. As the shots rang out, they must have awoken echoes of the building's dark past.

A PAGE FROM THE PAST

During the nineteenth century, some efforts were made to reduce the number of capital offences and to tackle the gross overcrowding and woeful conditions of Ireland's prisons. One obvious answer to both problems seemed to be to increase the number of convicted offenders sent overseas, as transportation to the penal colony of Australia had been available as an option for convicts from the late eighteenth century onwards. Australia was an empty continent – the Aboriginal population was small – and labour was needed to build the new British colony. There was no cheaper labour than convict labour, and the number of convicts sent to the Antipodes steadily grew during the first half of the nineteenth century. More convicts were sent to Australia from County Wicklow than from any other Irish county. In the early days, this may have been because the 1798 rebellion lasted longer in Wicklow than in other counties, but later on it reflected the willingness of Wicklow's judges and magistrates to send offenders overseas. Transportation was cheaper than imprisonment at home and it was readily resorted to in cases of long term sentencing. Indeed,

the minimum period of transportation was 7 years, but in practice it was usually a life sentence as those who left Ireland hardly ever returned. Many actually died en route to Australia, as conditions on board the convict ships were horrendous. The journey took 6–8 weeks and the convicts in the hold of the vessel suffered terribly. The cramped conditions meant that any type of infectious disease or sickness spread rapidly and only the strongest survived. Food rations were minimal also, leading to very high mortality rates on the ships. For example, the *Hercules*, which sailed for Australia in 1801, lost about a quarter of its complement of convicts on the voyage. A unique record of transported prisoners is provided by the transportation register for Wicklow gaol, which is still extant and kept in the National Archives of Ireland. Its pages tell many stories of heartache and misery and this section will examine just one page of the register. The page in question covers the period from March 1837 to March 1838. This was a time when the pressure of population growth led to farms being subdivided into smaller and smaller units, making it extremely difficult for the rural lower classes to eke out a living from the uplands of the Wicklow Mountains. As poverty and desperation increased in Wicklow, some of its inhabitants turned to crime. Those who were caught were likely to face transportation for even very minor crimes, as the transportation register reveals.

Convicts in the Gaol in the County of Wicklow

Names	Ages	Crimes	Sentences	When Tried	Before Whom Tried	When Transported	Date of Removal
			1837				
Patrick Butler	21	Larceny	7 years	Lent Assizes	Baron Foster		
John Walsh	12	Larceny	7 years	Lent Assizes	Do	Calcutta 18 April 1837	
John Fields	22	Larceny	7 years	Lent Assizes	Do	Do	
Hugh Fitzpatrick	32	Cow Stealing	Life	Lent Assizes	Do	Do	
James Mahony	(?)	Violent Assault	7 years	29 March	Do	Do	
John Power	24	Cow Stealing	Life	Summer Assizes	Capt. J. Dogherty		
William Cuddy alias Byrne	23	Sheep Stealing	Life	Summer Assizes	Do		
Patrick Byrne	25	Cow	Life	Summer Assizes	Do		
James Sharp	42	Horse Stealing	Life	Summer Assizes	Do		
James Hetherington	45	Sheep Stealing	Life	Summer Assizes	Do		
Edward Murphy	33	Larceny	7 years	28 June Sessions	Asst. Barrister		
Thomas Shannon	24	Felony	7 years	October Sessions	Do		Kilmainham 9 November 1838
Patrick Courtney	42	Larceny	7 years	October Sessions	Do		
			1838				
Patrick Byrne	41	Sheep Stealing	10 years	Lent Assizes	Judge Moore		6 March (infirmary)
Peter Kelly	26	Highway Robbery	Life	Lent Assizes	Do		
Charles Jones	27	Highway Robbery	Life	Lent Assizes	Do		

The faded page in the transportation register gives us an idea of the varied cross-section of crimes for which convicts were transported. Initial transportation from Wicklow was principally reserved for felons who had been convicted of political crimes related to the United Irish Rebellion of 1798, but transportation from Wicklow to the penal colony continued long after the 1798 period. The rebels who left Ireland aboard the *Tellicherry* in 1805 had many successors.

Men, women and children of and above the age of 7 years were held in Wicklow gaol, but there are no females listed in this extract. This does not mean that women did not commit crimes, or that they were never transported, for they did and they were! However, most transportees were males, and young males formed the largest proportion of the convict body. Excluding James Mahony (no age given), the average age of the convicts on this page is 28 years. Young men were the most likely group in society to become involved in crimes. The nature of the majority of the crimes listed here is indicative of the fact that Wicklow was a predominantly rural county, dependant on agriculture. Most of the crimes involve stealing of some kind or other, and many of them involve animal theft. There was much hardship in Ireland as a whole at this time and Wicklow was no exception. Population pressure in those pre-Famine days (by 1841, the population of Ireland was well in excess of 8 million people) meant that there was a rapidly growing cottier class, and continuous subdivision of small farms among the typically large families of the tenant-farmers meant that the cottiers and smallholders were being squeezed out and found it harder and harder to make ends meet. In these circumstances, some turned to crime and agrarian crime is a constant *motif* in nineteenth-century Wicklow. Young men of this cottier class were likely to have benefited from a recent subdivision of land as they came to marriageable age and started an independent life, but with an unviable smallholding. The cottiers' inheritance was a poisoned chalice, so they sometimes supplemented their meagre income with the proceeds of criminal activity.

The reaction to animal theft in this extract is interesting. The landlord-tenant system valued land. Land was life and the economy of rural areas depended on agriculture, and animals on the land represented wealth. Any threat to these animals – and to the agrarian status quo – was dealt with most severely. All the cases involving animal theft in 1837 merited transportation for life in the eyes of the bench. Patrick Byrne got a 10-year sentence for sheep stealing early in 1838, but he was one of the older men to be tried, at 41 years of age, and he may have been in ill health as, according to the register, he was removed from the gaol to an infirmary. This may account for the leniency of the sentence (if one can view 10 years as lenient!). On the other hand, James Mahony only received a 7-year sentence for violent assault.

Animal theft, which put wealth and property at risk, was perceived as a more serious crime and merited a longer sentence than injury to persons. Peter Kelly and Charles Jones

were both involved in highway robbery. Highwaymen were rare, but there are recorded cases. Captain James Freney operated as a highwayman in west Wicklow in the eighteenth century; his hideout was under a bridge in Hollywood Glen. Other highwaymen to operate in this area were named as O'Connor and Lawlor. Kelly and Jones were obviously carrying on a long-standing Wicklow tradition! Rural poverty could provide an underlying motive for the crime of highway robbery, and for the larceny cases that appear in the register. The term larceny is very general, so it is difficult to say much about these cases. Youth was evidently not seen as a reason for clemency, as 12-year-old John Walsh was transported for 7 years, exactly the same sentence as was given to his elder peers found guilty of the same crime. On the face of it, the case of Thomas Shannon is intriguing. The term 'felony' is not as specific as one might like, but given the fact that he was moved to Kilmainham Gaol, Dublin, it is probable that this felony was of a political nature. The rebellions of 1798–1803 were long past, and the Young Ireland rising was still a decade away in 1838, but the 1830s saw a nasty and sometimes vicious Tithe War played out in Wicklow. Tithe was a tax paid to the Anglican Church and everyone had to contribute regardless of their own religion. The standardisation of tithe collection was fiercely resisted and led to much agrarian violence. Men joined secret societies such as the Rockites to intimidate and terrorise anyone who paid the tithe. It is possible that Shannon was such a man, but the register is suggestive rather than specific regarding his membership of such a secret society. While it is a valuable primary source, the register can also be a bit infuriating at times because of the information that it does not give. In addition to being vague in relation to the actual offences, the register does not provide any home addresses for these men, who probably came from every corner of the county. What it does provide, however, is a fascinating insight into the criminal underbelly of County Wicklow during the nineteenth century.

A BLEAK BUILDING: WICKLOW'S HISTORIC GAOL

Wicklow's historic gaol stands at the centre of the county town and is a major visitor attraction today. Work commenced on the gaol in 1702 and it was opened shortly afterwards. Fr Owen McFee, a Catholic priest found guilty of saying mass, is the first known inmate. Thomas Ryves arrested McFee in 1714, and the 72-year-old priest was incarcerated in Wicklow Gaol while awaiting transportation to a British penal colony in America. Active, if sporadic, persecution of the Catholic clergy continued until about 1730, but the absence of further prosecutions in County Wicklow suggests that the following decades witnessed the demise, if not of the Penal Laws, at least of their strict enforcement. As the eighteenth century progressed, tentative efforts were made to reform the awful conditions in Irish prisons. Hygiene and sanitation were nonexistent in the overcrowded cells. In 1785 the prison reformer Sir Jeremiah Fitzpatrick MD visited Wicklow Gaol and stated that it was a 'very insecure bad prison'. Prison reform acts were passed in both the eighteenth and nineteenth centuries, but prison reform was a slow process.

From 1788 onwards, convicts were transported to Australia, and transportation of the inmates of Wicklow gaol continued until 1856. The failure of the 1798 rebellion and its aftermath ensured that large numbers of transportees left Ireland during this period. Over 140 Wicklow rebels were transported, including well-known rebel leaders such as Michael Dwyer, Joseph Holt, Arthur Devlin, Martin Burke, John Mernagh and Hugh Vesty Byrne. Later, prisoners were transported for a variety of crimes, ranging from stealing livestock, as was the case with Patrick Byrne, to infanticide, as was the case with Eliza Davis, who was actually sentenced to death for her crime but had her sentence commuted.

A new gaol building was completed in 1843, increasing the number of cells to seventy-seven. The Great Famine of 1845–50 saw a huge rise in cases of theft as starving people stole food to stay alive. Some people actually committed crimes in the hope of being incarcerated, as food rations in the gaol were better than those in the county's workhouses. One such case occurred in 1847 when Lawrence Murphy, a 14-year-old boy from Dunlavin, was charged with 'disorderly conduct in Baltinglass workhouse' and sentenced to 1 month in Wicklow gaol. As late as the summer of 1849, a resident magistrate noted that 'a great number of cases arose from robberies committed in the various workhouses with a view of getting sent to gaol where they are better fed'. However, conditions in the gaol during the Famine were appalling, and the number of inmates reached 780 at the height of the catastrophe.

Wicklow gaol was demoted to the status of bridewell for minor offenders in 1877 and the prison was officially closed in 1900. However, it reopened during the 1919–21 War of Independence. It also remained open during the Civil War. The most prominent prisoner during this period was Erskine Childers, who was held there before being moved to Dublin,

where he was executed. The gaol was finally closed in 1924. In the late twentieth century it was refurbished and opened as a tourist attraction. There were reports of ghostly sightings during the refurbishment, and today the grim building attracts paranormal investigators as well as people with an interest in Wicklow's history. Given its horrid history, the ghost hunting is hardly surprising!

5

WICKED WICKLOW WOMEN

Over the centuries, County Wicklow has produced many remarkable women, some of whom are not remembered fondly! Wicklow has had its fair share of murderesses, thieves, scarlet women, schemers, plotters and traitors. This chapter gives a brief account of two of these women.

ROSE O'TOOLE (O'BYRNE): THE MISTRESS OF INTRIGUE

Rose O'Toole (*c.* 1558–*c.* 1629) was the wife of Wicklow chieftain Feagh Mac Hugh O'Byrne, but was a formidable character in her own right. Born Rose O'Toole, she was the eldest daughter of Fiach and Rose O'Toole, the leaders of another well-known Wicklow clan. Rose married Feagh Mac Hugh in the 1570s. She was related to Captain William Basnett, constable of Wicklow Castle and this helped both herself and her husband by giving them a connection to the English authorities in Wicklow. Gaelic Irish clans sent their children to be fostered with other clans, and Rose was fostered by Thomas Garrahall of Ballelocha. Her marriage brought two indomitable spirits together, and from the outset the marriage was a tempestuous one. However, it meant that Rose abandoned her ties to the English authorities and joined her husband in his rebellions against the Crown. This alienated her from her father, who tried to keep on the right side of the English overlords. Fiach O'Toole implicated his son-in-law in an attack on Castledermot in 1575, but Rose cajoled her husband and persuaded him not to seek revenge on her father. However, relations between the two men remained sour until Fiach's death in 1578.

In August 1579, Rose played an active part in plotting to join Lord Baltinglass in an attempt to overthrow the English authorities. On 19 January 1580, Rose and Feagh met Lord Justice William Pelham and Rose in particular managed to convince him that the O'Byrnes were loyal subjects. It is probable that Rose used her physical attributes and feminine charms to help persuade Pelham of the O'Byrnes' peaceful intentions. All accounts agree that she was a beautiful, striking, intelligent and charming woman. In folk memory and oral tradition, Rose is depicted as a beautiful but wicked lady in a crimson cloak. During the Baltinglass revolt, Rose remained in remote Rosahane, deep in the Wicklow Mountains near Ballymanus. Rose's brother, Barnaby O'Toole, was arrested and this placed a severe strain on her marriage to and relationship with Feagh, who actually took a new wife to compensate himself for the loss of Rose's favours. Rose was a proud woman and this was a huge insult for her to bear. She was captured by English forces and in January 1580 she made a statement accusing Feagh of collusion with Lord Baltinglass and Gerald Fitzgerald, Earl of Kildare, in plotting against the Crown. The authorities were delighted with Rose's change of heart, putting it down to the wrath of a woman scorned. Eventually Rose was released and she returned to Glenmalure, where the English hoped she would be in a position to provide them with valuable information about Feagh.

Rose had a hard job to convince Feagh of her *bona fides* on her return. Moreover, she was feared by many of the clan members and their allies, so she had to build up their trust as well. Feagh's sons, in particular, did not welcome their stepmother back into the fold. Despite this, Rose's position was secured when Feagh stood by his estranged wife as long as she was loyal to him, and she again became a valued and valuable member of the Glenmalure clan. Feagh recognised Rose's skill as a political negotiator and as an envoy whom he could send to other clan chieftains. She was, in fact, a consummate politician in her own right and again her wiles and charms served her well in her endeavours. Her reputation spread among the leaders of Munster and Ulster, and the English authorities now employed spies to report on the activities of their one-time spy. These spies provided information about a growing rift between Rose and her stepsons, particularly the eldest, Turlough. The ongoing feud and open hostility between Rose and Turlough created familial difficulties for Feagh. Childless Rose was determined that Feagh should not be succeeded by Turlough, who she feared might banish her from his lands or even imprison or execute her. Rose threw her weight behind the claims of Feagh's other sons Phelim and Redmond, both of whom were married to her own younger sisters, in the hope that these bonds of kinship would work in her favour. However, Feagh did not heed Rose's campaign against Turlough. Despite the fact that leaders, including the great Hugh O'Neill of Tyrone, were deeply impressed by Rose's political skills, she had become a divisive figure in her own clan and its stronghold in Glenmalure.

The authorities continued to distrust Feagh and tried to stir up trouble for him among his rivals, including Rose's own clan, the O'Tooles. In 1588 Turlough O'Byrne met Phelim O'Toole of Powerscourt, but the parley quickly descended into bitter recriminations on both sides. O'Toole had to flee the meeting in fear of his life, and the O'Byrnes proceeded to devastate the O'Toole lands of Fercullen, putting more strain on Rose's position within the O'Byrne camp. Rose's brother Barnaby also had a rocky relationship with the O'Byrnes. This became evident during the first escape of the Ulster chief Red Hugh O'Donnell from Dublin Castle. O'Donnell sought shelter with Phelim O'Toole when he reached the Wicklow Mountains, and Rose was present when O'Donnell arrived at Castlekevin.

By rights, Phelim should have held O'Donnell and informed the authorities of his whereabouts. Rose proposed a novel solution for the dilemma. She suggested that a fast messenger be sent to Feagh Mac Hugh O'Byrne at Glenmalure so that he could come and spirit O'Donnell away, and a slow messenger be sent to Dublin Castle so the English would arrive only to find that the bird had flown. The ploy seemed to fulfil Phelim's duty to the authorities while ensuring that O'Donnell would actually escape. The plan was adopted.

'The best laid plans of mice and men gang aft agley' however, and things did not go to plan. The plotters did not reckon with the Avonmore River being in flood. Feagh and his comrades could not reach O'Donnell and the government troops arrived first. Red Hugh was recaptured and the whole affair tainted relations between the O'Byrnes and the Ulster chieftains, while also adding to the pressure on Rose and the strain between herself and her husband, who was publicly embarrassed by the incident. However, Red Hugh escaped again in 1591 and was rescued, suffering from exposure, in the mountains by the O'Byrnes. It was Rose who nursed him back to health and she played a pivotal role in nurturing the relationship between the young Ulster chief and her husband. Rose was now playing a central role in her husband's plotting and scheming, and in 1594 Adam Loftus, Archbishop of Dublin, was accused of entertaining her at his house for seditious purposes. In January 1595, Rose, Feagh and their followers had to flee for their lives during a surprise attack led by Sir William Russell on Glenmalure.

The renewed attacks by the English bore fruit when Rose was captured by Sir Henry Harrington in April that year. She was taken to Dublin to stand trial for treason and, if found guilty, she would be burned at the stake. Faced with such a dreadful prospect, Rose offered to turn informer. On 5 May 1595, a letter to Lord Burghley stated that Rose had offered to help the authorities to take down Feagh's son, Turlough O'Byrne, but she could not be persuaded to play a part in the capture of Feagh himself. In that month also, Rose was found guilty of treason and sentenced to death by burning. Russell, however, now persuaded Rose that Turlough was plotting against his father, and asked her to move against her stepson. Rose needed no persuasion! She was allowed to warn Feagh of the alleged plot. Feagh arrested Turlough and offered to exchange him in return for Rose's release. This came to pass when Turlough was sent to Dublin for trial and Rose was released but not pardoned – the threat of her sentence was left as an incentive for her future loyalty. Turlough was executed on 18 July 1595.

With Rose and Feagh reunited, they began plotting rebellion again. However, their relationship was now more strained than ever, particularly as Feagh was hearing rumours that Turlough had, in fact, been innocent. Rose's role was integral to Turlough's fate and Feagh realised that Rose may have duped him to save her own skin. All the O'Byrnes distrusted her and the Turlough faction openly despised her. Feagh wanted to avenge Turlough and he used Rose's political skills to try to repair the damaged links between himself and the O'Tooles. An alliance between the two clans was agreed in 1596 and the O'Byrnes entered the Nine Years' War later that year. However, the war went badly for the clan, and a series of attacks by Russell threatened Rose and Feagh, who narrowly escaped capture in November. Rose was despatched to negotiate with Sir Henry Harrington and Sir William Harpole, constable of Carlow Castle the latter of whom was actually accused of sheltering Rose during the attacks on Glenmalure. Rose was to be Feagh's envoy at peace talks on 17 April 1597, but on 8 May Feagh was discovered in a cave and killed by English soldiers. Rose was recaptured and on 3 July she was again sentenced to be burned at the stake. She was held in a cell in Dublin Castle to await execution.

Rose now made a number of offers to the authorities in order to save herself from an awful fate a second time. She now offered to take down her stepsons, Phelim and Redmond. Ironically, both were also her brothers-in-law. They had fled to Ulster following their father's death but were trying to gather a force large enough to return to Wicklow and reclaim their inheritance. Another costly campaign in Wicklow was the last thing the authorities wanted and they could see the attraction of Rose's offer. Rose was released on 7 January and pardoned on 1 February 1598. She had evidently learned from being unpardoned before! Phelim submitted to the English in 1598; neither he nor Redmond were aware of Rose's treacherous offer to betray them. Even so, tension grew between them and their stepmother, who no longer wielded the same power and influence following the death of her husband. In 1599 she left Glenmalure and remained exiled from the O'Byrne clan until her death. Details of her later life are sketchy. She was living in Dublin in 1606, but her past evidently caught up with her as she was a prisoner in Carlow Castle in 1610, where she would remain until her death some time in the late 1620s.

Rose O'Toole (O'Byrne) was a hugely influential figure during her lifetime. A woman in a man's world, she used all her skills, charms, talents and instincts to become a major political player in her own right. A born survivor, she was willing to betray her stepsons and other close friends to avoid a fiery fate – which she did, despite being sentenced to death on three separate occasions. Her beauty and intelligence were both renowned. Her legend lived on after her death. Two hundred years after the death of Feagh, visitors to Glenmalure from France heard folk tales of the beautiful, enchanting, wicked woman of Wicklow, whose crimson cape matched the colour of the blood on her hands!

CROPPY BIDDY DOLAN: THE REVOLTING REBEL

Brigid Dolan was born in the south Wicklow village of Carnew in 1777. She was a child of the poorer classes; her father was a thatcher by trade. He was often absent doing roofing jobs away from the family home and Brigid's mother was allegedly a remote woman, devoid of maternal affection. Lack of parental interest in the child resulted in her growing into an unruly teenager, noted for her wild behaviour and fraternising with visiting itinerant tinkers when they came to the village. She kept company with boys rather than girls and, unusually for a girl at that time, learned to ride very well. As a child she rode donkeys, graduating to horses as she matured. She became a fine horsewoman and this ability meant that she could travel and keep up with rebel units during the rebellion of 1798.

Brigid Dolan became interested in the United Irish movement, an organisation established to bring about political reform and put an end to the inequalities in Irish society. She was uneducated and illiterate – surviving copies of her signature reveal a simple X – and it is unlikely that she had any deep understanding of the great political issues of her time. It is far more likely that her links to the United Irish movement were for the sake of popularity and acceptance in a rural settlement where many of the young men of her class joined the movement. Accounts of her life stress the sexual misdemeanours and blasphemous language which she used freely. Such behaviour would have made her a social outcast and she entered into a life of prostitution, which ensured that she was further shunned by many people. However, she was eventually employed as a domestic servant by William McCormick of Carnew. McCormick later joined the local yeomanry when it was formed to defend the country against the dual threats of a French invasion and a United Irish uprising. Brigid Dolan then left his employ, possibly because she realised that her flirtation with the United Irishmen would be likely to cause trouble in a Loyalist household such as McCormick's. Though not a full-blown member of the organisation, it is likely that Brigid took the oath of secrecy of the United Irishmen, so she may have been in possession of knowledge regarding the personnel and activities of United Irishmen in the locality.

Carnew was a base of the hard-line Loyalist faction in Wicklow before and during the 1798 rebellion. A pre-emptive massacre of suspected United Irishmen in Carnew ball alley marked the zenith of ultra-loyalism in the area during the early days of the rebellion. This and the harsh treatment meted out to suspected rebels in the run up to the rising ensured that there were reprisals against the Loyalist community once the rebellion broke out in the area. Brigid Dolan joined the rebels when they seemed to be gaining the ascendancy in the Carnew region. The rebels cropped their hair tightly, giving rise to the nickname 'croppies', and Brigid became known as 'Croppy Biddy Dolan'. She was with the insurgent forces from early June – she was at Gorey in County Wexford when the Wicklow rebels commanded by Billy Byrne of Ballymanus arrived there – to late August. Women were not usually active participants in the rebel army, but there were some exceptions. Brigid's skills on horseback may have made her useful as a combatant, but it is unlikely that she was. She did have a horse, however, and women were certainly engaged as messengers and as nurses. Brigid herself never claimed to be a combatant, but would not say what she actually did during the rebellion. Her claim that the men gave her provisions during this time led to allegations that she plied her trade as a prostitute among the rebels, but in view of the lack of evidence this is difficult to prove or disprove.

Following the rebel defeat at Vinegar Hill, Brigid remained with the rebels in the field and seems to have struck up a relationship with their leader, Joseph Holt of Roundwood. Some accounts of rebel activities at this time refer to Holt's 'public intercourse with ... the notorious Bid Dolan'. When Holt's wife Hester arrived in the rebel camp, Brigid Dolan left it. Eventually in late August 1798 Brigid Dolan, her rebellion over, returned to Carnew. She was arrested in Coolkenna in September and offered to give evidence against rebels and former rebels in order to save herself. She was a valuable witness and the authorities eagerly accepted her offer. The ultra-Loyalist Thomas King of Rathdrum welcomed Brigid Dolan as a potential informer and witness in his campaign to round up rebels and to negate the pardons that had been granted to some of them by using new evidence against them. Brigid Dolan named rebels and pointed the authorities in the direction of the mountain hideouts of many fugitives who remained on the run. According to some accounts, she even accompanied the cavalry units sent out to capture such men. So began Brigid Dolan's new career – that of prosecution witness.

Brigid recognised the fact that assisting the victorious authorities would work in her favour. Just as she joined the rebels when it seemed they would carry the day with a military victory, she also wished to be identified with the winning side and helped the authorities to identify rebels. One writer has suggested that whenever she was invited to appear as a witness for the prosecution, Brigid was willing to swear to anything that she thought would please the Orange party, who supplied her with money and whiskey. There is no doubt that her evidence was often flimsy, fabricated and full of holes. It is entirely possible that she was actually told what to say in a number of trials, although there is no extant documentary evidence to support this. On the other hand, many of her statements were clearly false and made with the sole intention of implicating the defendants. She claimed, for example, that the Wicklow leader Garret Byrne was at Vinegar Hill in Wexford on 21 June 1798. This is patently untrue. She was also present at the trial of Garret's brother, Billy Byrne of Ballymanus. It is difficult to say with any certainty whether her evidence resulted in his execution. Certainly, Billy Byrne was publicly hanged in Wicklow town, but Brigid Dolan was not the sole witness against him. We can say that she played a part in the guilty verdict, but how important her evidence actually was is difficult to quantify.

What can be quantified are Brigid Dolan's appearances as a witness. From the summer of 1799 and her first evidence given in Rathdrum, she made damning allegations on numerous occasions. She was particularly involved in trials involving the reprisal killing of Loyalists in both Wicklow and Wexford. Her evidence was possibly rehearsed, differing from that of other witnesses because it was always very detailed, leaving the court in no doubt as to the guilt of the accused, although there may have been doubts as to its veracity! In the trial of John Fowler for murdering Roger Pierce, for example, Brigid Dolan stated that Fowler served with the rebels. He rode a bay horse and was armed with a sword and a case of pistols. He was present when Pierce was piked by a number of rebels and she stated that Fowler stabbed the fallen Pierce with his sword to finish him off, while a priest stood by and watched the murder. She was also positive that she saw Fowler giving orders when the rebels burned the village of Carnew. Such evidence is compelling and damning and only one verdict could be expected. Over and over again, Brigid Dolan gave such evidence!

During this time Brigid Dolan was in receipt of money, new clothes and a supply of alcohol. There is no doubt that her work as a prosecution witness was supported by the state. During the summer of 1800, with Brigid still freely giving detailed and damning evidence, the Grand Jury foreman William Hoare Hume, MP from Kiltegan asked the viceroy to consider (perhaps reconsider would have been a better word) the use of Brigid Dolan as a court witness. The sheer volume of her evidence and her almost total recall of events that she could only have witnessed for a few seconds two years previously was becoming an embarrassment and undermining her credibility in and out of court. Following her retirement as a star witness, she was actually pensioned off with money from the secret service funds of Dublin Castle. She received £22 15*s* in 1801, 1802 and 1803. No longer of use to the authorities, Brigid Dolan returned to Carnew.

Following her return to her home village, Brigid Dolan was more of an outcast than ever. She was shunned like a leper of old by the Nationalist, Catholic community. A contemporary local ballad about Billy Byrne of Ballymanus, which she must often have heard on the lips of local people, assured the listeners that the Devil had 'a warm corner for ... Bid Dolan'. Ostracised by the Catholic community, Brigid Dolan was, in later years, dependant on the 'poor box in the Protestant church'. Nationalist accounts of her autumn years are vitriolic and reports of her falling on hard times are unmistakably triumphalist in tone. Illness and loss of her mental faculties may well have been her lot, but the extremely biased nature of the sources in which this is recorded makes the story open to doubt. What is certain is that she was never forgiven by the Nationalist community for her part in betraying many of her former colleagues and condemning them to the hangman's noose. Only a few facts regarding her later life are reasonably certain. She had a child some time after her court days, but never married. She was in fear of the local Nationalist community and procured two bulldogs for her protection. She was taunted, jeered and even stoned by local Catholic children in her home village. When she died aged 50 on 29 October 1827, she was buried in the Church of Ireland cemetery – the only member of her family and extended kinship network not to be interred in the Catholic graveyard. The separation, rejection and exclusion from former family, friends and neighbours that was so apparent in her lifetime continued even after her death. Croppy Biddy Dolan was not easily forgotten.

Brigid Dolan has become a hate figure in Irish nationalist history. Given her actions, this is an understandable response, but the real woman is more complex than the biased caricatures might suggest. There were familial and social reasons for her wild childhood and immoral teenage years. She did accompany the rebel army for a long period of time, and certainly spent more time in rebel camps than many of the more famous female Nationalist heroines. Most of the better known Nationalist 'women of '98' actually spent very little, if any, time with rebels in the field. However, Brigid Dolan's lack of moral compass and suspicions that she engaged in prostitution have meant that the longevity of her rebel career has been both overlooked and forgotten. Coupled with this was the clear absence of political motivation for her rebel activities, a fact that came very sharply into focus following her decision to give evidence – probably both true and false – against many of her former comrades. This act, more than any other, ensured that the rebel Croppy Biddy was replaced in Wicklow folk memory by the monstrous Bid Dolan, the turncoat. When Ireland gained its independence and began to honour its historical heroines, Bid Dolan was not among them. Although she spent a long time with the insurgents, remaining with Joseph Holt after many others had left him, she was not and could never be included in the roll of honour of the women of '98. Her treachery made her unsuitable for Nationalist Ireland. Her loose morals made her unsuitable for Catholic Ireland. The independent Ireland that emerged in 1922 was both Catholic and Nationalist in character, and its version of history and historiography reflected this fact. Bid Dolan, the hate figure, became a mere caricature, and a serious study of her life and significance was not carried out for many years. There is no doubt that she was a complex character, but to many she remains Bid Dolan, the informer, a woman who got what she deserved in her later life, a woman whose name is reviled and repugnant, a woman who was perhaps the most wicked of all wicked Wicklow women!

6

POOR PARNELL: WICKLOW'S WRONGED LEADER?

Throughout Irish history, there have been two separate but often intertwined movements working to achieve independence from Britain. One was the physical force tradition, in which armed insurrection was the avowed aim of Irish rebels. The other, lesser known but perhaps more successful, was constitutional nationalism, whereby the Irish cause was furthered by working within the existing political system. In the late nineteenth century, constitutional nationalism was dominated by the question of Home Rule, which sought to establish an Irish parliament in Dublin, and the leader of this movement was one of the most enigmatic of Irish patriots; a man whose name is still divisive in some Irish households; a man whose legend has grown over the years and a man who hailed from County Wicklow. He was Charles Stewart Parnell.

CHARLES STEWART PARNELL: THE UNCROWNED KING OF IRELAND

Oh, have you been to Avondale
and lingered in its lovely vale,
where tall trees whisper and know the tale
of Avondale's proud eagle?

(Dominic Behan, *Avondale*)

Incredibly, the fate of the British Empire once depended on the whims of a Wicklow landlord! Charles Stewart Parnell from Avondale House just outside the village of Rathdrum was the leader of the Irish Home Rule Party during the 1880s. Home Rulers wanted to re-establish a separate Irish parliament in Dublin. The old Irish parliament had been abolished by the Act of Union, which came into force on 1 January 1801. The old parliament had been exclusively Protestant, but the nineteenth century had witnessed Catholic Emancipation and by its later decades Roman Catholics were playing a leading role in Irish politics. Parnell, a Protestant himself, led a largely Catholic party which controlled the political balance of power in London at a time when the British Empire covered more than a quarter of the globe and was at the zenith of its power. The decisions of the Home Rule Party could make or break governments, and the larger British parties, the Conservatives and the Liberals, both tried to woo the Irish Home Rulers with promises of land reforms, electoral reforms and, eventually in the case of the Liberal Party led by William Ewart Gladstone, the introduction of Home Rule for Ireland and the establishment of an Irish parliament in Dublin.

Charles Stewart Parnell was the son of a Protestant landlord, born into comfortable surroundings in Avondale House, Rathdrum, County Wicklow. After a wayward early career, he entered parliament in 1874. There he met Michael Davitt, and this fateful meeting gave the young Parnell what he had been sadly lacking up to that point – a purpose in life and a cause with which he could identify. Davitt's background was as different to Parnell's as one could imagine. Davitt's childhood was one of abject poverty and of hard labour in an English textile mill, where he lost an arm in an industrial accident at a young age. Later on Davitt joined the Irish Republican Brotherhood (also known as the Fenians) and served time in jail for his involvement with this secret oath-bound organisation. However, once they met, Parnell and Davitt were quick to understand each other, and mutual respect sprung up between them as they were both involved in a long and bitter campaign to arrange an amnesty for Fenian prisoners. Davitt even tried to persuade Parnell to join the Irish Republican Brotherhood. Parnell declined the invitation to join, but he was interested in enlisting the support of the Fenians for his own political career, as he had already joined the Home Rule Party, then ineffectually led by Isaac Butt. Michael Davitt went to America, and gained the support of the exiled Fenian John Devoy, the leader of the American branch of the organisation known as Clan na Gael, for a grand coalition of Fenians, land agitators and Home Rulers. This was known as the New Departure, and was an alliance of revolutionary and constitutional nationalists who vowed to work towards land reform first and then to turn their attention to the question of Home Rule.

THE LAND LEAGUE

The New Departure was cemented with great success in 1879. Parnell probably had little interest in land reform *per se*, but he shrewdly recognised the importance of gaining the support of Ireland's farmers and agricultural workers in the struggle for Home Rule that lay just over the horizon. Ireland was a predominantly rural country and whoever had the support of Ireland's rural heartland had a clear mandate from the majority of the Irish people. Butt's health was failing and Parnell was the party's rising star as well as the obvious successor to the leadership. Davitt knew that Parnell was the best man to successfully lead the new movement. The truth of this was shortly borne out by Butt's death in 1879 and Parnell's becoming leader of the Home Rule Party in 1880. Davitt recognised the importance of having an instantly recognisable figurehead, so when he founded the Irish National Land League, he deferred to Parnell when the presidency of the league was being decided. Having Parnell as the president of the Land League contributed enormously to its success. Davitt was the chief organiser and was excellent in this role, but Parnell became the face of the movement and the voice of its members. The combination of Parnell and Davitt, whose skills were so different but whose talents complemented each other so well, ensured the success of the ensuing Land War. Once committed to the Land League, Parnell devoted all his time and energy to the movement. Parnell's great achievement was the ability to unite all shades of Nationalist opinion behind one banner. Land reformers, moderate constitutional nationalists, Home Rulers and Fenians answered Parnell's call to join the Land League. Clan na Gael provided financial aid, and the influx of US dollars gave the Land League real clout, as the support of the Clan quickly developed into support from all sections of Irish nationalist opinion in America. The support of the Catholic parish clergy, along with many of the Catholic bishops, also gave the movement respectability and provided a solid basis for support in the rural areas, which were more under the sway and influence of the clergy than in the more cosmopolitan urban areas. The Land League quickly went to work, fighting for the 'Three Fs' – fair rent, free sale and fixity of tenure – on Irish farms. It organised resistance to the landed elite, and many landlords suffered as a result of falling foul of local Land Leaguers. The Land League was arguably the most significant mass movement in modern Ireland, and the huge support it received from right across the whole spectrum of Irish nationalism uniquely equipped it for success in the Land War of 1879–82.

Irish farmers began a campaign of land agitation that eventually led to violence against landlords. However, the Land League was not an illegal organisation, although it sailed close to the wind on occasion. Parnell urged tenants to 'keep a firm grip on their homesteads' and he encouraged the use of the boycott, a form of social exclusion named after its first victim, Captain Charles Boycott. The British government had severe difficulties in understanding the tactics of the League and were unable to deal with them effectively. The Land League itself never openly encouraged violent or illegal activity, and was even involved in charitable work among the Irish rural poor, such as building temporary wooden houses for evicted tenants and their families. Nonetheless, the activities of the League and the agrarian unrest in Ireland contributed to the downfall of Benjamin Disraeli's Conservative government in the general election of April 1880, which put Gladstone's Liberals back in office. The election was Parnell's first electoral triumph and he now led an increasingly militant Irish party in the London parliament. William Edward Forster, Gladstone's chief secretary, attempted to lessen tensions in Ireland with the introduction of the Compensation for Disturbance Bill. However, the House of Lords would not accept this bill, so existing land laws were enforced against Irish tenants. This escalated the Land War and agrarian violence increased as the country awaited the introduction of a new land bill by Gladstone's Liberal government.

The violent situation and the power vacuum created by agrarian instability saw the Land League implement its own law to rival that of the government. Tenants now went to courts organised by the League, thus effectively paralysing the British government and the representatives of the Crown in Ireland. The League courts dealt out stronger sanctions to errant tenants than the courts of the state itself, so no one would occupy the lands of evicted tenants, thus causing landlords' losses to mount still further. In response to this challenge to its authority, the government introduced strict coercion acts and moved against the leadership of the League. Davitt was the first leader to be arrested. However, in 1881 Gladstone also introduced a new land act which granted most of the demands of the League and which introduced the principle of dual ownership of the land by landlords and tenants. Fixed, fair rents were to be decided in a new special land court. Irish landlords did not agree with this system, and its introduction was one of the first indications that they would end up as the losers of the Land War in the long term. Initially, the Land League insisted that peasant ownership was the only acceptable principle of settlement and refused to end the agitation. They claimed that the act did little or nothing for the poorest tenants, especially those existing on the breadline (such as those in the upland areas of Wicklow) and that it ignored tenant farmers in arrears with their rent, who were precisely the people who were most vulnerable and who needed the most protection.

THE KILMAINHAM TREATY

Gladstone met the failure of the League to accept the 1881 land act head on, and ordered the arrest of its principal leaders, including Parnell, Dillon, O'Brien, Brennan, Sexton and Kettle. He then went further and suppressed the league itself. However, not to be outdone, the Land League was replaced by a new organisation, the Ladies' Land League, which Davitt had established before his arrest. The Ladies' Land League ably took up the work of the movement where their male counterparts had left off. Parnell warned that 'Captain Moonlight' (i.e agrarian violence) would take over the situation. His prophecy proved correct, and the Ladies' Land League was unable or unwilling to control certain wilder elements involved in the agitation. Rural violence was spinning out of control, forcing Gladstone to negotiate with Parnell, who was now languishing in Dublin's Kilmainham Gaol. These negotiations led to Gladstone and Parnell agreeing the Kilmainham Treaty of March 1882, which brought an end to the agitation. In effect the treaty ensured that Parnell would accept the terms of the 1881 act, gave some more minor concessions to tenants (though those in arrears were still excluded) and, crucially, obtained Parnell's agreement to disband the Land League and to take no further interest in land reform. For his part, Parnell realised that the landlord system was well on the way to being wiped out in Ireland, and also had personal reasons for wishing to get out of prison at this time. He had been conducting a liaison with a married woman, Katharine O'Shea, in England and she had just borne him a child, which died shortly after its birth. Parnell wanted to be with Katharine and the signing of the Kilmainham Treaty generated much goodwill in Britain, although it also marked the end of the New Departure, as many hardliners saw the document as a sell-out to Britain.

Four days after the Kilmainham Treaty, another act of violence in Ireland destroyed much of the goodwill in Britain and left a scar on Anglo-Irish relations. Chief Secretary Foster refused to accept the Kilmainham Treaty and resigned. Lord Frederick Cavendish replaced him. Cavendish, however, was murdered along with the under-secretary, T.H. Burke, on his arrival in the Phoenix Park by a secret society known as the Invincibles, which had links to the Fenians. In a knee-jerk reaction, Gladstone introduced a new Coercion Act. However, this new act did not alter Gladstone's attitude towards Parnell, and did not prevent him from fulfilling the promises he made in the Kilmainham Treaty. This paved the way for later land acts such as the Ashbourne Act of 1885, the Balfour Act of 1891, the Wyndham Act of 1903 and the Birrell Land Act of 1909. Bit by bit, these eroded the power of the landlords and eventually created the conditions which allowed for peasant ownership. The advancement of loans to tenants eventually led to the abolition of landlordism and Ireland became a land of owner-occupiers. Parnell saw the destruction of landlordism as a first step on the rocky road to Home Rule for Ireland.

FIGHT FOR HOME RULE

With the Land War well on the way to reaching its inexorable conclusion, Parnell turned his attention to the Home Rule question, which dominated the remainder of his life until his premature death in 1891, and continued to dominate Irish politics for decades afterwards. Characteristically, Parnell threw all his energy into the new project. The National League replaced the Land League. It drew its support from the same nationalistic sources as the Land League, but it was firmly controlled by the Irish Home Rule Party. The new mass movement provided the national political machinery that had been absent up to this point, and it enabled the Irish party leaders to control the choice of all candidates for elections. When Parnell also promised to fight for the introduction of separate Catholic education under the proposed new Dublin parliament, the Irish Catholic Church threw its not inconsiderable weight behind the new campaign. Parnell insisted on strict party discipline and ran a tight political ship. The Irish Home Rule Party had to sit, act and vote together as a unit. Thus the party was the first in the world to implement the political party whip system. Parnell also recognised the value of holding the balance of power. The election of 1885 was significant, for it resulted in a resounding Parnellite victory in Ireland and a less conclusive Liberal victory in Britain. The balance of power had become a reality.

The huge Irish support for Parnell and the narrow margin between the principal British parties tipped the balance. Gladstone wanted to achieve a solution to the Irish problem, and a mixture of principle and pragmatism finally converted him to the cause of Home Rule. In return for the support of the Home Rule Party, Gladstone offered to introduce a Home Rule Bill for Ireland and the promise of the Holy Grail was enough to bring Parnell and his party off the fence. The Irish Party entered into an alliance with the Liberals, and Gladstone's Home Rule Bill of 1886 tried to introduce a measure of justice to the governance of Ireland. Parnell's tactics and Gladstone's inherent trust of Parnell's essential conservatism had won the day, but the new bill posed some problems too. The introduction of such a bill meant British refutation of the policy by which Ireland had been governed previously, and recognition of the claim to nationhood by Ireland. The Conservative Party bitterly opposed the bill. No allowance was made for the Unionists of Ulster, who did not aspire to Home Rule. This was to prove a step too far even for some of Gladstone's own Liberal followers. Gladstone was aware of the Ulster problem, but he believed that the 'upper chamber of the new Irish government could be weighted in favour of the Unionists and could safeguard their interests'. A minority of Liberals, led by Joseph Chamberlain, did not agree and voted against the bill, which was defeated by thirty votes in the House of Commons.

The government fell, and this setback meant Gladstone had to call the general election of 1886, which was the first of its kind to be fought in Britain on the issue of Home Rule. Gladstone was defeated, but he hoped to return to office soon and successfully to introduce Home Rule.

Meanwhile, Parnell faced another crisis. A special commission of three high court judges inquired into *The Times* publication of a series of articles entitled 'Parnellism and Crime' in 1887. *The Times* printed highly incriminating letters condoning the Phoenix Park murders of 1882, supposedly written by Parnell. However, the investigation into the matter found that Richard Pigott, a disreputable Dublin journalist, had forged the letters. Parnell was vindicated, his popularity soared to new heights and Gladstone invited him to visit the Liberal leader's home at Hawarden. It was like a state visit – and all boded well for the introduction of Home Rule in the not too distant future.

FALL OF PARNELL

However, within a year, a heavy blow fell. Parnell's affair with Mrs O'Shea was like a ticking time bomb and the momentum Parnell gained from the Pigott verdict was wiped out by his appearance in the divorce court concerning his adultery with Katharine, the wife of Captain William H. O'Shea, a former member of the Home Rule Party. Victorian morals were outraged and Parnell was painted as a philanderer and homewrecker of the worst kind. Lurid details of clandestine meetings emerged and society's righteous indignation at these sexual shenanigans increased with every new revelation. Many of Gladstone's puritanical non-conformist Liberal followers were utterly appalled by the affair, while the reaction of British non-conformist opinion to the O'Shea case was of vitriolic hostility towards Parnell's continued leadership of the Irish Party. Although Gladstone's campaign for Home Rule was perceived as a just cause by these non-conformist elements, their shock and enmity towards the leader of the Home Rule

Party now overruled everything else. In their eyes Parnell had to go, and Parnell and Gladstone had become so directly linked in their pursuit of Home Rule that Gladstone's own position, the entire Home Rule project and the leadership of the Liberal party were now under scrutiny. However, Parnell refused to resign, even temporarily, although this course was strongly recommended by Gladstone and many others, including the imperialist Cecil Rhodes.

The Home Rule Party was thrown into disarray. After intense meetings of the Irish MPs, who were in a quandary, and a critical denunciation of Parnell by the Catholic hierarchy, the majority of the party members rejected Parnell's leadership. A minority of Irish MPs still supported him, but he began to show progressively more irrational behaviour, such as his violent denunciation of the Liberals. The Irish party split, but the Parnell faction was repeatedly defeated in a number of by-elections during 1891. Ironically, extremists such as the Fenians rallied to him as his leadership style became more extreme, but overall public opinion had changed. Parnell wore himself out in his final campaign and his health suffered irrevocably. He returned to England and married the love of his life, the recently divorced Katharine, but 5 months later, on 6 October 1891, he died in her arms. He was only 45 years old. His funeral, to Dublin's Glasnevin cemetery, was one of the biggest ever seen in Ireland, with huge crowds attending from all parts of the country and from all walks of life. Divisive he may have been, but now that he was dead, the ordinary people of rural Ireland wanted to pay their respects to their uncrowned king, the man who had spearheaded the Land League long before his Home Rule Party split apart.

With the fall of Parnell, the Irish party was deprived of a leader whose genius was irreplaceable. His career was like a meteor streaking across the heavens and his fall seriously damaged the Home Rule cause. Parnell's stubborn refusal to take temporary retirement had forced his party into action, and that party was now bitterly divided. It would be a decade before it was tentatively reunited under the leadership of John Redmond, and two decades before Irish Home Rule returned to the mainstream political agenda. Yet Parnell's accomplishments as a statesman, although damaged by his fall from grace, were not completely destroyed. Arguably his most significant achievement was that he managed to demonstrate that both Irishmen and women were capable of efficient, continual and valuable political action in and out of parliament. He proved to many sceptics in Britain and elsewhere that Ireland was deserving and capable of self-government. Although Parnell eventually failed in his pursuit of Home Rule, his control over politically motivated mass movements saw the birth of the modern party political system and bore fruit in Irish politics a generation later.

Perhaps when all is said and done, it is the myth of Parnell as the wronged leader that lives on in popular memory. The Irish people are generally kind to the memory of Parnell. He erred and he was punished for it. He was, in many ways, the architect of his own downfall. Yet few other leaders in Irish history were as highly respected or as dearly loved by Irish Catholics as this Protestant. A landlord who helped Ireland rid itself of the landlord class, Parnell had remarkable political instincts and Gladstone, perhaps the only comparable contemporary statesman, regarded the Irish leader as 'an intellectual phenomenon'. Parnell was the political colossus of his age, towering above the Irish politicians whom he created and even eclipsing the British politicians with whom he interacted. Parnell's intense hatred of anything English, his extreme speeches and his memorable fall seem to obscure memory of his more moderate achievements such as the alliance with the Liberal Party or the Kilmainham Treaty with Gladstone. Parnell's role in the success of the New Departure, the Land League, the National League and his creation of a political Home Rule machine were all significant achievements in their own right. The latter particularly had implications for nationalist Irish political parties such as Sinn Féin and Fianna Fáil in the twentieth century.

One of the most prominent monuments in the city of Dublin today is located at the northern end of O'Connell Street, at the very heart of the city centre. It commemorates Parnell and is inscribed with the words he used when giving a speech in Cork in 1885, words which have become indelibly linked to the leader and synonymous with his name:

> No man has a right to fix the boundary to the march of a nation. No man has a right to say to his country 'Thus far shalt thou go and no further'. We have never attempted to fix the ne plus ultra to the progress of Ireland's nationhood and we never shall.

Parnell's contribution to the making of modern Ireland lives on in the populist memory, and the memory of this truly remarkable Wicklow landlord and his life's work remains both vibrant and powerful, especially in his native county.

AVONDALE HOUSE

Today Avondale House is open to visitors, who will see a rich collection of Parnell memorabilia and catch a glimpse of the lifestyle enjoyed by Ireland's landed elite during the nineteenth century. The house was built in 1777 for a wealthy barrister named Samuel Hayes, who was known as 'the tree man of Avondale' because he began extensive planting around the house and wrote the first ever book on Irish forestry. The Parnell family acquired the house in 1795 and it was here on 27 June 1846, when the Great Irish Famine was ravaging the surrounding area, that Charles Stewart Parnell was born. The Parnells continued the improvements to the estate, and continued the tree planting begun by Hayes. Today Avondale House is inextricably linked to the story of Irish forestry and houses the headquarters of *Coillte*, the Irish national forestry body. Avondale was purchased by the state in 1904 as a centre for silviculture and the first plots of trees laid out in the pattern of a continental forest garden. Today the forest park at Avondale, on the west bank of the Avonmore River, contains many rare trees within in its tranquil 214 hectares, and includes several marked walking trails, with numerous shady nooks in which to rest along the way. The house and forest park are well worth a visit; after all, where better to contemplate the rise and fall of Charles Stewart Parnell than here, 'where tall trees whisper and know the tale of Avondale's proud eagle'?

7

TRIAL AND RETRIBUTION: THE ONLY BLACK AND TAN EXECUTED IN IRELAND

In 1920, due to a shortage of Royal Irish Constabulary (RIC) recruits in Ireland at the height of the War of Independence (also known as the Anglo-Irish War), the British authorities began to recruit RIC members in Britain. A shortage of uniforms meant that the new force was dressed in khaki jackets and black trousers, earning them the nickname 'Black and Tans'. An officer class, the 'Auxiliaries', were also recruited. Contrary to Irish nationalist propaganda, most of the 'Tans and Auxies' were not recruited from English jails, but many of them had been in the British army during the World War One. They carried out many atrocities, but only one of them was ever executed for a crime. That crime took place in west Wicklow, in the townland of Milltown near the village of Dunlavin. The Milltown murder caused a sensation in its day and the trial that ensued was followed closely by everyone on the island of Ireland.

EVENTS AT MILLTOWN HOUSE

On Monday 18 April 1921, a Black and Tan named William Mitchell pleaded 'Not Guilty' to the charge that he did 'at Milltown, Dunlavin, County Wicklow, on 2 February, murder Robert T. Dixon J.P.' at a court martial in the City Hall in Dublin. He was then alternatively charged with manslaughter and once again he entered a plea of 'Not Guilty'. It was also alleged that RIC Constable Hardy had accompanied Mitchell during the fatal attack, but Hardy had committed suicide in Dunlavin RIC station the next day. This meant that Mitchell was tried alone. Mitchell was defended by counsel and so the case of the Milltown murder began.

When the prosecution opened the case, the prosecuting counsel laid out the facts as they were known. Robert T. Dixon was a farmer, an auctioneer and a magistrate for the district. The counsel knew of no reason why Dixon's house should be targeted, or he murdered on the night in question. Dixon's murder had occurred at approximately 12.30 a.m. At about that time, a loud knocking was heard at the door of Dixon's home, Milltown House. The son of the murdered man came downstairs in his slippers, and despite no lights being on in the house, he could see two figures outside in the moonlit night through the glass panel in the door. When he asked who was there, they answered 'Military' and demanded that the door be opened. The young man asked them to wait until he got dressed. He went back upstairs, alerted his father and returned to the door armed with a poker from the fireside. However, when he opened the door the two men, whose faces were covered, used a flashlight and brandished revolvers, before asking for money. Robert Dixon, the father, was by now in the hall and he took money from his trouser pockets. Despite this, the intruders demanded more money and began to threaten both the father and son.

The men fired a shot in the hall. At this point Robert Dixon went upstairs, but one of the men followed him. The prosecuting counsel contended that this man was RIC Constable Hardy, and that, while on the stairs, he fired the shot that would prove fatal to Robert Dixon. Meanwhile, Dixon's son had been wounded twice and was lying on the downstairs floor. At this point the two ladies in the house attacked the intruders with sticks, causing them to run away. One of the ladies then cycled to Dunlavin to notify the authorities and to fetch a doctor. When Dixon's house was searched, two hats were found.

These hats belonged to Constables Hardy and Mitchell. A flash lamp which was used in Dunlavin RIC barracks was also found, as well as spent bullets from service revolvers.

On parade the next day, Mitchell's revolver was found to be 'fouled' as if it had recently been fired and Hardy's revolver was revealed to have bloodstains on it. The court was informed by the head constable that twenty rounds of ammunition were also missing. The civilian clothing of the accused and of his companion were found to be bloodstained and the prosecuting counsel summed up by telling the court that, even if he had not fired the fatal shot, because he accompanied Hardy on the fateful night and because of his intent, Mitchell was equally guilty in the eyes of the law and he asked the court to find him so.

The son of the murdered man confirmed the prosecuting counsel's opening statement, adding that once inside the house the men had called out for a light and the reason that Robert Dixon had gone upstairs was to fetch this light. One man followed his father upstairs and the second man, who remained in the hall, flashed a light in his face. This second man produced a revolver and told the witness to put down the poker which he was holding behind his back. The witness put down the poker, but he then seized the intruder and grappled with him. The intruder called to his comrade upstairs for help as he struggled with the witness.

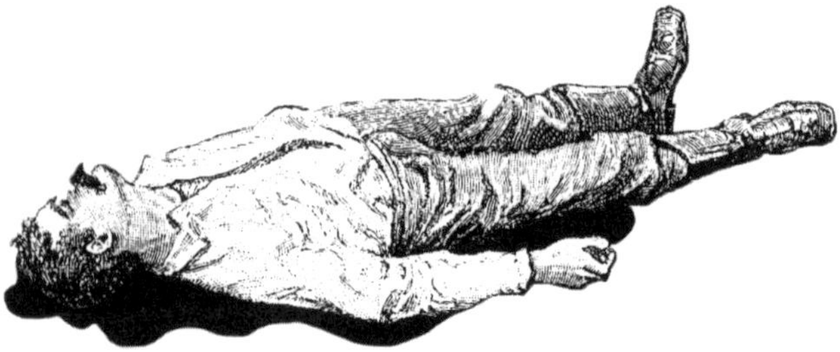

The other intruder came down the stairs and the witness told how he continued to grapple with the second intruder, trying desperately to keep the man in the line of fire between himself and the man who had come back downstairs. This man called out, 'Let me get at him till I have a good shot at him'. The witness then told how the man had come closer and had pointed the gun at him over the shoulder of his comrade. The witness continued, 'With my right hand I grabbed the revolver [of the man I was struggling with] and pushed it behind his back. The man who was struggling with me shouted at his comrade not to shoot. I managed to wrest one revolver away and stepped back, but the man who had come down the stairs fired and struck me in the left shoulder. I also fired, but my gun did not go off. The man fired again and shot me in the hip. I fell and heard more shooting, but got up again and went for one of the men. I fell a second time and one of the men rushed over to me and hit me on the head with the butt of his revolver'. The witness also said that the second man (referred to as B) had a moustache and wore grey clothes. Under cross-examination, the witness told how, when one of the ladies of the house attacked one of the men with a stick, he shouted 'Mother, let me go'!

The dead man's daughter was the next to give evidence. She described how the men entered the house and how she saw her aunt hitting the man who was struggling with her brother in the hall with a stick. She told how she had tried to get one of the men by the throat but couldn't, so she took a stick from the hallstand and attacked him with it. However, he took the stick from her and she got another, but shots were then fired and she saw that her father was badly wounded. The witness said she got her father onto the sofa and her brother sitting in a chair before getting dressed and cycling to Dunlavin for the doctor. As she was dressing she looked out of the window and saw the two men outside, striking matches and apparently looking for something on the gravel. One man constantly called the other 'Bill'. When the witness returned with the doctor, she found the flash lamp on the table and two hats on the floor. She told counsel under cross-examination that one man left the house slightly before the other and in reply to a question from the judge advocate, she said that she saw smoke coming from one of the men's revolvers, but she was not sure how many shots had been fired.

The next witness was the dead man's sister, who told the court that when her brother had told the men that he would fetch a light, one of them said 'Bring down the wife and kiddies'. The witness was on the second landing of the stairway and she heard a shot just before her brother stepped onto the stairs. After the shot, she heard her nephew below call out 'Father, Father' and then everyone went downstairs into the hall, where she saw a man grappling with her nephew. The witness hit the man on the head several times with a stick and blood was pouring down his face. He struggled with her for the stick, shouting 'Mother, mother, have pity! Let me out'. The witness then opened the door and the man fled, followed by the second man a few seconds later. When the intruders had gone, Robert Dixon collapsed on the couch, saying 'I am done'; he was bleeding heavily from the stomach. Her nephew was propped against the mantelpiece and he was unable to do anything, as he was very faint. On the following day, a district inspector showed her the corpse of a dead constable in Dunlavin. The prosecuting counsel asked if she had identified the dead constable, to which she answered, 'Yes, he was one of the men in my brother's house the previous night'. The witness said that the torch and hats produced in the court did not belong to any member of the Dixon household. In reply to the judge advocate, the witness said that the dead constable was the man who had been on the stairs with her brother on the fateful night.

MEDICAL EVIDENCE

The court martial heard the medical evidence next. The doctor told the court that he arrived at Milltown House at about 2 a.m. on the morning of 2 February to find Robert Dixon lying on the sofa. He had been shot in the chest and in the stomach.

One wound was 3 inches below the left nipple, a second wound was 1 inch lower than this and a third wound was found over the right nipple. The second wound had also produced an exit wound as it passed right through Dixon's body. The doctor remained with his patient, who died about an hour later. Robert Dixon's son had wounds in the left shoulder and about the hips. He was operated on, and was in a very critical condition. The bullet was still in the young man's shoulder.

POLICE EVIDENCE

The police evidence followed. The court was told that the police reached Milltown House at about 5.30 a.m. and Robert Dixon was lying dead on the sofa. His son was critically injured in an upstairs room. Bullet marks were found on the walls of the hall and a police sergeant found a flash lamp of the type that was standard RIC issue as well as both spent and live bullets. The police returned to Dunlavin at about 9 a.m. The police in the station were instructed to parade and to produce their revolvers and ammunition. When Constable Hardy was examined, he was found to have a fresh cut on his forehead and another cut, 1¼ inches long, on the top of his head. When the station bicycle shed was examined, it was found unlocked. Constable Hardy's revolver was bloodstained, and Hardy could not produce his civilian hat. Furthermore the accused man [Mitchell] was found in possession of a 'fouled' revolver. He did, however, produce a civilian hat. The police witness went on to relate how both Constables Mitchell and Hardy were relieved of their arms, ammunition and accoutrements and placed under police supervision.

While in Dunlavin barracks, Constable Hardy committed suicide by shooting himself with a service revolver. He was later positively identified by Robert Dixon's sister as one of the intruders at Milltown House. At this point Constable Mitchell was arrested and charged that he, along with Constable Hardy, did murder Robert Dixon and attempt to murder his son at Milltown, Dunlavin on 2 February 1921. Mitchell made no reply when cautioned, but upon examination he was found to have a fresh cut about 1 inch long on the top of his head. When searched, Mitchell was found to be in possession of one farthing. When cross-examined by the counsel for the defence, the police witness said that no man from Baltinglass had been identified as one of the Milltown raiders. He stated that the accused was placed in an identity parade and had been picked out along with another man. However, the other man was from Wicklow town, not Baltinglass, and had been chosen specifically because of his resemblance to the accused. The torch found at the scene was identified as one that had been in use in Dunlavin barracks for about a year.

The police witness went on to say that cartridges from a service Webley revolver had been found in the hall of Milltown House. A cartridge from an automatic pistol had also been found, in addition to the bullet holes in the walls. The witness told the court that there were bloodstains on the coat sleeves and trouser legs of the accused's clothing and that twenty rounds of ammunition were also missing from the barracks strong room, near the day room. Fourteen policemen were stationed in Dunlavin barracks, some being English and some Irish. None of them had been given permission to remove any of the 571 bullets stored in the strong room. This figure included some ammunition for automatic weapons. Some of the police in the barracks used to take a drink, but they had been advised to give it up and there was no indication of heavy drinking during the night in question.

A police sergeant who had been on duty on the night of 1 February told the court that he returned to Dunlavin barracks at 11 p.m. When cross-examined, the sergeant told the court that he had never seen the sign of drink on the men in Dunlavin barracks. They were sober in carrying out their duties for king and country. On the night in question, he had the torch that had been identified for the court martial with him and he left it on the shelf in the day room. When he was going to bed, he noted Mitchell and Hardy standing in the kitchen and the hall. He testified that a piece of leather from the torch had been found under the matting in Dixon's house. Some bullets and the two hats produced to the court were found at the same time. These articles were all handed to a police analyst. The police analyst was called and told the court that he had examined Constable Hardy's blue suit and Constable Mitchell's grey suit, two velour hats and a revolver. With the exception of one hat, all of the articles showed traces of human blood.

The barrack orderly at Dunlavin barracks on the night of 1 February deposed that the accused told him he was leaving the barracks after the 10 o'clock roll call. The witness told him that this was against regulations. Later on, the accused came into the day room and said that he was going to the strong room to get some wood. The accused spent about half a minute in the strong room, where the ammunition was kept. Constable Hardy also went into the strong room a little later on. At about 11.30 p.m. the witness saw three constables, including Hardy and Mitchell, in their room drinking bottled stout. The witness said that they offered him a drink, but he refused it. At about midnight, Hardy asked the witness for the flashlight as he wanted to go to the rear of the barracks. The witness duly identified the torch in the courtroom. Later on, the witness heard an iron door, such as the one fitted to the accused's room, being opened. He and another constable went to investigate and he told the court that they found the accused's room empty. Some time after 1 a.m. the witness heard voices coming from the accused's room and heard a light motorcar passing on the road outside. The next day, Mitchell asked the witness what he had told the County Inspector and the District Inspector. He told the accused that he had reported that nobody had left the barracks on the night of 1 February. The accused seemed relieved to hear this.

The witness then identified the hats in court as the property of Constables Mitchell and Hardy. The witness had joined the RIC in London on the same day as the accused and knew his hat by the amateurish way in which the band had been put onto it. Under cross-examination, the witness said that the accused had been sometimes referred to as 'Mitch'. On the night in question, the three constables who had offered him a drink were under the influence of alcohol as their eyes were glossy. The witness did not think that Hardy and Mitchell were on bad terms or that Hardy had ever threatened Mitchell with a gun. The witness told the counsel for the prosecution that the accused was not drunk on the night in question.

Following an adjournment, the barrack orderly was recalled to the witness stand and identified the flashlight to the court. Another constable corroborated the evidence of the barrack orderly, saying that he had heard the sound of the iron door at about 12.15 a.m. He was with the barrack orderly when they found Mitchell's room empty. Later on, he heard the iron door again and the sound of feet moving. He also heard the voice of the accused, which was raised, as if he were excited. On the following day, Constable Hardy was missing from parade. During a search of the barracks, the witness entered Hardy's room and found him lying on his left side. He was obviously dead. A recently fired revolver was lying on the bed and there was blood flowing from Hardy's chest. In reply to the counsel for the defence, the witness stated that the accused had taken some drink on the night in question but was not staggering about. Two other police witnesses identified the accused's hat

and one of them added that he had never seen him wear it on the street, but it was unusual for the police to wear mufti in public, except when they were on special duty.

Another constable testified that the accused and Hardy had woken him up during the night. They were both wearing civilian clothes and the accused did not speak to the witness when he entered the room. Under cross-examination, the witness denied that he was very drunk that night, but admitted that he had taken some drink. He could not explain why Mitchell and Hardy had entered his room and left it again. He had recognised them by the firelight in the room. The witness told the court that Hardy had to pass through the witness's room to reach his own room. In reply to the judge advocate, he said that Hardy and Mitchell had given him a bottle of stout that night and both constables had been in suits when they were drinking with him.

The court heard that the bicycle shed at the rear of the barracks had been locked up at 5.30 p.m. on 1 February. There were three bicycles there and the key was hanging in the kitchen. At 9 a.m. the following morning, the police witness found the shed open and noted bicycle tracks in the yard. The tyres of two bicycles were wet and the bicycles were not as clean as they had been the evening before. The key of the shed was also not hanging in the place where he had put it. The witness told the judge advocate that the tracks led from the back gate to the shed door. The court was also told that a Webley cartridge was found about 500 yards from Milltown House on the road, which was not very wet at the time.

EVIDENCE FOR THE DEFENCE

At the request of the defence counsel, a statement taken from the accused on 7 March was read to the court. In it Mitchell stated that on 1 February he had called into a public house in Dunlavin, where Constable Hardy was well known. He had heard that Hardy was involved in a row in the public house and he wanted to make enquiries about the matter from a young lady, who refused to tell him what the row was about. She said that Hardy was mad and had threatened her with a revolver. He asked the young lady if she wished to take the matter further, but she refused, saying that she would not give evidence against anyone. Mitchell said that he had been drinking in the morning, and that in the afternoon he had returned to the public house to try to persuade the young lady to see the head constable. However, she refused to do so. He continued drinking that evening and ended up in the hotel beside Dunlavin barracks. He could not remember being on roll call that night, but did remember talking to some other constables in the barracks. He could not remember leaving the kitchen that night.

The next thing that he remembered was being woken up early on the morning of 2 February by someone shouting 'Get up. They're here', or words to that effect. When he got up, he found that all the Irish police had left the barracks, leaving the English men behind. Everyone was confused and he was told that someone had been shot. Nevertheless, he went back to bed until about 8 a.m. The constables were later asked to parade in the day room and to bring their guns, ammunition and civilian suits with them. The district inspector kept his property and he did not know that he was under supervision, but he was arrested the following day. He had taken part in three identification parades, but, to the best of his knowledge, he had never been identified. Mitchell stated that he had always tried to avoid Constable Hardy, as he was a violent man who had been warned several times about taking his revolver out. He had only been in Hardy's company about three times, always on patrol. Hardy had asked him to lend him some civilian clothes, but Mitchell had refused. However, when Hardy said he was going to Dublin on 6 February, Mitchell relented and said that Hardy could have a loan of his civilian clothes. Mitchell stated that he had fought in France for 3 years during the Great War. He had been nearly killed in the Battle of the Somme in 1916 and had been wounded again in 1918, before being pensioned off. Since the war, drink affected him badly, causing him to suffer with his nerves and making him suggestible and easily influenced. He was 33 years old and married. His wife was expecting a child. He had been among the first in England to volunteer to join the RIC and he ended his statement by saying that he had joined with good intentions, to prevent this sort of thing and not to provoke it. The defence and prosecution counsels addressed the court and the judge advocate summed up before the court formally closed.

When the court reopened, the president of the court stated that the accused was found not guilty of the second or alternative charge of manslaughter. Then the president asked if there were any character witnesses to speak for the accused. A police witness was sworn in and testified that Mitchell had joined the RIC in November 1920 and was transferred to Dunlavin on 1 January 1921. He was a clean and apparently sober man and no complaints had been brought against him. He discharged his police duties efficiently and well. The counsel for the defence produced documentary evidence that Mitchell had spent 4 years in the army and, according to his commanding officer, he was a smart, intelligent, steady man and a hard worker. The president asked the accused if he wished to address the court, but Mitchell did not. The court closed again and the charge of murder was considered.

GUILTY OF MURDER

In the event, Mitchell was found guilty of the murder of Robert Dixon and of the attempted murder of his son. The sequel to the trial of William Mitchell was short. He was removed to Mountjoy Gaol and there, on the morning of 7 June 1921, was hanged by the neck until dead in accordance with the sentence of the court martial. No other Black and Tan was ever executed for any crime during or after the War of Independence. Perhaps it was the background and social status of the murdered man that sealed Mitchell's fate. Robert Dixon was an affluent Protestant magistrate. One may speculate that this was the real reason why the trial took place, but for Irish Nationalists, the true significance of William Mitchell's execution lies in the fact that at least one member of the Crown forces paid for a crime committed during the Anglo-Irish War. He is buried in a plot within the walls of Mountjoy Prison in Dublin, and is now largely forgotten, despite the sensational nature of his court case at the time.

8

THE ANGLO-IRISH TREATY OF 1921: THE WICKLOW CONNECTION

Between the years 1919 and 1921, Ireland was in the throes of a bitter struggle as the IRA engaged in a guerrilla war against British Crown forces. The conflict, known as the Irish War of Independence or the Anglo-Irish War, engulfed the whole island and County Wicklow was no exception. Local IRA attacks began with sniping at police barracks to intimidate the officers inside, and boycotting members of the RIC in the area. The IRA also threatened and intimidated people who co-operated with the RIC. The IRA ambushed RIC patrols in the countryside and staged attacks on barracks, often burning them down to ensure that they could not be reoccupied. By the end of the guerrilla conflict in Wicklow, the IRA had cleared the countryside and forced the RIC to withdraw to the larger towns where they had the support of the British military. Once the IRA began their campaign in Wicklow, hardly a month passed in which there was not some incident or form of aggression towards the Crown forces. Attacks by the IRA temporarily drove the RIC out of several rural areas, for example around Rathdrum and Dunlavin. In June 1919 IRA attacks were carried out in both Newtownmountkennedy and Bray. Between June and July that year, the IRA burnt out five barracks in County Wicklow, including those at Ashford and Roundwood. Baltinglass was also a very active region throughout the War of Independence. On 24 January 1920, an attack on the barracks resulted in the death of an RIC constable, and there were many raids in and around the town throughout the war. Ambushes and attacks permeated the county. In February 1921 there was an ambush on a combined RIC and military patrol in Bray. As the war dragged on, these attacks became larger in scale and more frequent. On 13 May 1921 there was sniping at patrols in both Bray and Enniskerry, and this sniping later spread to many barracks in the east of the county. The RIC raided suspected IRA volunteer hideouts and safe houses for munitions and explosives, but the mountainous terrain in rural parts of the county made such operations difficult. The IRA attacks did not stop in the later stages of the war, even though it was evident the conflict was nearing an end with talk of a truce in the air. On 27 May 1921 a well-organised attack was carried out on Tinahely barracks. The attackers had cut off the town, felling trees to block roads and cutting telegraph wires to thwart communications. In June 1921 it was reported that a flying column was operating in the Hollywood/Donard area. However, neither the military nor the RIC sent out any patrols to investigate the report, pointing perhaps to the sapping effect that the ambushes, raids and attacks were having on their morale. The War of Independence ended when a truce came into force in July 1921. It was obvious that difficult negations lay ahead, and later that year Ireland sent its envoys plenipotentiary to London to partake in talks with a view to finding a permanent solution to the Irish problem and signing a lasting treaty with Britain. In the absence of Eamon De Valera, the Irish delegation was led by Arthur Griffith, although its best-known member was probably Michael Collins. Two other members of that delegation had strong links to County Wicklow. They were Robert Barton and Erskine Childers.

ROBERT BARTON

Robert Barton, the son of Protestant and Unionist parents, was born in 1881 to Charles and Agnes Barton of Glendalough House, Annamoe, County Wicklow. The family owned a large estate of over 1,500 acres in Wicklow and their wealth was further enhanced by their interest in the famous French wineries of Barton and Guestier. Barton received a classic English public school education at Rugby School before graduating from Oxford and, later, the Royal Agricultural College, Cirencester, England. He introduced many agricultural improvements on his estate in Wicklow, and his tenants benefited from the new agricultural methods he employed. He also worked for the Irish Agricultural Organisation Society and was deeply involved in the co-operative movement. In 1908, while on a tour of co-operatives in the west of Ireland, the Unionist Barton became convinced that Home Rule was the way forward for Ireland. However, when the First World War began, Barton joined the Royal Dublin Fusiliers as a commissioned officer. Although two of his brothers were killed in the First World War, Barton resigned his commission in the wake of the 1916 Easter Rising in Dublin.

Robert Barton was in Dublin that week and was deeply impressed by the attitude of the captured rebels in the aftermath of the rising. His own understanding and charitable attitude to the rebels and their families caught the attention of Michael Collins, who advanced Barton's name within the Nationalist faction. In the general election of December 1918, Barton was elected MP for west Wicklow and his first mission was to accompany Michael Collins, George Gavan Duffy and Sean T. O'Ceallaigh to Paris in an effort to meet with US president Woodrow Wilson during the Paris Peace Conference, which was to end with the signing of the Treaty of Versailles. Barton's international diplomatic credentials were further underlined at the first meeting of the breakaway Sinn Féin Irish parliament in Dublin, the Dáil, when he read out their 'Message to the Free Nations of the World'. His academic and practical farming background made him the obvious choice as the Dáil's first Minister of Agriculture. He began the huge task of land redistribution in Ireland by setting up the National Land Bank.

In February 1919 Barton was arrested and imprisoned by the British authorities. He found himself in Dublin's infamous Mountjoy jail on charges of making a seditious speech and uttering threats at Carnew, in the south of County Wicklow. On 16 March Barton was involved in one of the most daring and audacious prison breaks ever carried out in Ireland. Fellow Republican Richard Mulcahy had managed to smuggle a file into the prison, and Barton was sprung from the jail when a rope ladder was thrown over the 20-foot-high outer wall. Barton coolly left an effigy of himself in his bed and a note for the prison governor, stating that he felt that he had to leave due to the discomfort of his present surroundings! He remained on the run for nearly a year, but was recaptured in January 1920 and tried by court martial. He was incarcerated in Portland prison, where he suffered much at the hands of the warders. His support at home did not wane, however, and he was elected chairman of Wicklow County Council in his absence! The convict chairman was released in July 1921 and was immediately involved in negotiating the truce on the vessel of General J.C. Smuts in Kingstown (now Dun Laoghaire) harbour to end the War of Independence, which he co-signed with General Nevil Macready on 11 July at Dublin's Mansion House. Barton's popularity increased and he was elected MP for Kildare-Wicklow in the second Dáil of 1921–3, becoming the Minister for Economic Affairs. In that role it was always likely that he would be involved in the treaty negations with Britain, though even he could not have foreseen how much of a key player he would turn out to be in that long, bitter and tangled saga. He accompanied Eamon De Valera and Eamonn Duggan to London for preliminary talks in the summer of 1921, but De Valera and the British prime minister, David Lloyd George, had a personality clash right from the beginning and these talks came to nought. They did, however, increase the perception that Barton was very closely aligned with De Valera within the internal machinations of Sinn Féin.

When the full Irish delegation left Dublin for London later that year, Barton was one of three cabinet ministers on the boat. Michael Collins endorsed his inclusion, and ostensibly Barton was picked for his economic expertise. However, the British government perceived him as a De Valera puppet and they tried to marginalise him from many aspects of the negotiations. A rift developed between Barton and the head of the delegation, Griffith, who was suspicious of the ardent Republican Barton's insistence on 'external association' between Britain and Ireland – an idea propounded by De Valera as a means of avoiding membership of the British Commonwealth for any new Irish state that might emerge. Barton's attitude enraged Lloyd George, who referred to him scathingly as a 'pipsqueak', but he also annoyed Griffith, who felt that he 'created the wrong atmosphere' in talks on Anglo-Irish trade. Despite many setbacks, a treaty was eventually hammered out and Lloyd George gave the Irish delegation a blunt message – sign or go back to Dublin and back to war!

Lloyd George's ultimatum came with a time limit: the treaty had to be signed that night or not at all. So began one of the most dramatic and significant nights in Irish history, one in which Barton was to be a pivotal figure with a central role. Collins knew that the IRA were very low on volunteers, supplies and ammunition and so in no position to renew the War of Independence, let alone win it. Hence, he favoured signing the treaty. Arthur Griffith and Eamonn Duggan supported him in this position. Erskine Childers, the secretary of the Irish delegation, was against signing it. George Gavan Duffy wavered, letting it be known that he would allow himself to be guided by Robert Barton's decision. Thus it transpired that, in effect, Barton had the casting vote among the Irish delegates, for they all had to sign the document in order for it to be accepted. Lloyd George had warned of 'immediate and terrible' war should the treaty be rejected. As Barton agonised over his Republican principles, Duggan warned him that he might be hanged from a lamppost in Dublin if his intransigence led to the resumption of war. Enough young men had sacrificed their lives according to Duggan, and any gains made in the negotiations were in danger of being lost if the war-weary and weakened people of Ireland were plunged into a new conflict. Three times that night Barton stopped the other members of the delegation from going to Downing Street to sign the document. Three times he relented and eventually emotional stress and peer pressure told, with Barton reluctantly agreeing to accept the treaty document as a means of averting more bloodshed. Encouraged by Childers (who, as secretary, did not have to sign the treaty document), he had been the last man to hold out, and it was past 2 a.m. when he finally caved in to the enormous pressure. Barton's decision to sign made the Irish Free State a reality, paved the way for an Irish republic and shaped the twenty-six county Ireland that we know today.

However, it was also instrumental in bringing about the Irish Civil War of 1922–3. The treaty was passed in the Dáil, but a minority of its members, led by De Valera, refused to accept it and rejected the democratic vote of the Dáil. They went further, rejecting democracy itself and engaging in a civil war with the newly elected government led by Griffith and Collins. On his return from London, Barton had pilloried De Valera for his absence from the treaty negotiations, claiming that the divisive situation that now existed was De Valera's own fault. Barton voted for acceptance of the treaty in the crucial Dáil vote, but intriguingly, in a move demonstrative of the deep soul searching going on within him, he then joined the anti-treaty side in the civil war that followed. He took part in the fighting in Dublin and was among the group of anti-treaty 'Irregulars' who occupied the Hammam Hotel in O'Connell Street, the principal thoroughfare of Ireland's capital city. Having escaped from Dublin following the defeat of the anti-Treatyites there, Barton was chosen as Minister for Economic Affairs in De Valera's council of state, a shadow body set up in opposition to the elected pro-treaty government. In November 1922, the Barton family home was raided and Barton's cousin Erskine Childers was arrested and later executed. Barton survived the civil war but lost his Dáil seat in the general election of August 1923. It was the last election he would ever contest. He retired from active politics, brooding over his role in the signing of the treaty and in the disastrous civil war that followed. So consumed was he by his momentous decision to sign the document that he later wrote that he often wished that he had died in Portland prison rather than lived to take part in 'these cursed negotiations' that had cost so many lives.

Despite his retirement from the political arena, Robert Barton returned to public life when De Valera's Fianna Fáil party came to power in 1932. He had always been a close friend of De Valera, and the new taoiseach made him a director of the Irish Press, the Fianna Fáil-oriented newspaper that was seen as the voice of De Valera in the Irish Free State. Sean MacEntee also appointed Barton to the board of the Agricultural Credit Corporation (ACC), a state-sponsored body established to give cheap loans to Irish farmers. He became chairman of the board of the ACC in 1933, a position he retained until 1959. Barton did not put himself forward as a candidate, but ardently campaigned on behalf of Fianna Fáil during the 1933 general election, claiming that the signatories of the Anglo-Irish Treaty had been misguided and tricked into signing by promises that nationalists in the North of Ireland would have a say in the redrawing of the border between the North and the Free State. In 1934 Barton also became the chairman of the Turf Board, and remained in this post after the board had been altered and renamed Bórd na Móna in 1946. Coal shortages during the Second World War did much to encourage the development of the bogs during the war years, and it was decided to harness and utilise the Irish bogs in the aftermath of the Emergency, as the war was known in neutral Ireland. As chairman of Bórd na Móna, Barton did much to develop the resource, especially in the Irish midlands, until his retirement in 1960. Now in his twilight years, Barton lived to a ripe old age, before dying on 10 August 1975. To the end of his life, he was haunted by his decision the sign the treaty.

ERSKINE CHILDERS

Robert Erskine Childers was born in London on 25 June 1870. His family was related to the Bartons of Annamoe; Robert Barton's aunt Anna had married Robert Caesar Childers and Erskine, as he was known, was a child of this union. When Erskine was only 6 years old, his father died and he moved to Wicklow to live with his cousins, the Bartons. Childers' mother died in 1883, so the young Erskine Childers and Robert Barton grew up together and shared a close bond that was to become a lifelong friendship. Robert Barton acted as best man at Erskine's wedding. Childers attended Haileybury School and graduated with a first in law from Trinity College, Cambridge in 1893. The politically minded Childers became joint assistant clerk in the House of Commons in January 1895. An avid imperialist, Childers served in the British Army as an artillery driver during the Boer War. Following this conflict, Childers rose quickly to fame due to the success of his novel *The Riddle of the Sands* in 1903, which is widely acknowledged as the first example of the modern spy novel. A keen sailor himself, Childers' book tells the story of a British yachtsman who discovers a huge German naval threat to the Royal Navy in the run up to World War One. On 5 January 1904, Childers married Molly Osgood of Boston, Massachusetts. Although disabled, Molly was strongly anti-imperialist in her views, and she exerted a huge influence over her husband's political opinions.

In 1909, when the question of Home Rule for Ireland was again to the forefront of British politics, Erskine Childers became convinced that the Irish cause was a just one and became a supporter of Home Rule for the land in which he had grown up. In October 1910 he resigned his position as a senior clerk in the House of Commons, and in 1911 he published a political pamphlet entitled *The Framework of Home Rule*. When the third Home Rule Bill was passed in 1912 Unionists, who were not in favour of the new proposal, began to organise themselves to resist its implementation, especially in Ulster.

A clandestine anti-Home Rule army, the Ulster Volunteers, was formed and they smuggled in a consignment of guns and ammunition through the port of Larne on 24 April 1914. In the meantime, a similar pro-Home Rule military organisation, the Irish Volunteers, was also formed. Childers was concerned at the lack of effort on the part of the British authorities to stop the Larne gun-running, so he organised a shipment of guns from Germany for the Irish Volunteers. He used his own yacht, the *Asgard*, to transport these weapons, which were landed in broad daylight at Howth, County Dublin on 26 July 1914. Childers' maritime expertise contributed to the success of the venture, but the authorities did move against the Irish Volunteers who received the weapons. The different attitudes adopted by Crown forces in the face of Unionist and Nationalist gun-running were not lost on Childers and his colleagues. For a while, it looked as if civil war might break out in Ireland, but the implementation of Home Rule was postponed when the First World War began.

Despite his anti-imperialist stance, Childers supported the British war effort. He became a member of the Royal Naval Air Service, an arm of the Royal Naval Volunteer Reserve. He was involved in planning and intelligence operations, and was awarded the DSC in April 1917. Three months later he was released from military operations and appointed assistant secretary to the Irish Convention, a last desperate attempt to salvage Home Rule as the mood of Nationalist Ireland changed to favour a republic in the wake of the 1916 Easter Rising and the execution of many of its leaders immediately afterwards. The convention collapsed amid bitter recriminations on all sides early in 1918 and the following year, when the war was over, Childers made the fateful decision to return to Ireland, where he intended to use his political and literary skills as a propagandist for the newly resurgent Sinn Féin party.

Childers travelled to Paris in July 1919 to further the Irish cause at the international peace conference, but without much success. Woodrow Wilson's principle of self-determination for small states only applied to nationalists within the vanquished nations, and not to nationalists within the victorious ones, it seemed! Later in 1919, Childers, whose family had left an opulent life in Chelsea for a dangerous existence in Dublin, began to write for a nationalist publication, the *Irish Bulletin*. Childers' conversion to hard-line republicanism can be traced in his writings, such as his pamphlet *Military Rule in Ireland*, and from this point onwards his life and work would be totally devoted to the cause of Irish freedom. The arrest and incarceration of his cousin Robert Barton only served to strengthen his hard-line attitude, as did the atrocities and reprisals carried out by British forces, including the notorious Black and Tans, during the Irish War of Independence of 1919–21.

Although an ardent Republican at this stage, Childers found himself under suspicion by many of his comrades. He had the ear of De Valera and his ideas helped to shape some of the Dáil president's policies, but Arthur Griffith disliked and distrusted Childers, whom he referred to contemptuously as that 'damned Englishman'. Childers showed the zeal of the convert and, in Griffith's eyes, this led him to overcompensate by being too radical in his ideas. Other Republican leaders shared Griffith's mistrust of Childers and, given his background in the British intelligence services, many openly suspected him of being a spy planted in their ranks by the British authorities. They thought that Childers' hard-line zeal may have been a mere front to mask possible clandestine espionage activity. Despite the hostility directed towards him by some members of the leadership, he was appointed director of propaganda when Desmond Fitzgerald was arrested in February 1921. Childers' literary skills and the support of De Valera were crucial in this appointment, and Childers used his post as propaganda maestro to legitimise the IRA as the real army of Ireland, approved by and under the control of the legitimate Irish parliament, the Dáil, at every opportunity. Childers joined the Dáil himself when he was elected a Sinn Féin TD in May 1921.

Following the end of the War of Independence, De Valera's trust of Childers meant that he accompanied the first group of Irish envoys, led by De Valera himself, to go to London. When these preliminary talks yielded nothing, De Valera ensured that Childers travelled to London for a second time later that year, making him secretary to the plenipotentiaries led by Griffith. Crucially however, he was not a full member of the delegation as the signature of the secretary was not required on the treaty. During the protracted and intricate negotiations that followed, Childers kept De Valera personally informed on as many matters as he could. However, the British delegation distrusted Childers, perceiving him as a turncoat and a traitor, and they sought to marginalize him from the negations, establishing meetings with Collins and Griffith in order to exclude him at every opportunity. Consequently, tensions arose between Childers and the Griffith-Collins faction, and relationships were strained to breaking point as the signing of a treaty loomed ever closer. In the final hours before the treaty was signed, Childers pleaded, cajoled, begged, appealed, threatened and reverted to Republican rhetoric in a vain attempt to persuade the signatories, particularly his cousin Robert Barton to whom he cited family connections as emotional blackmail, not to sign the document. All to no avail – the treaty was signed and later it was accepted by a majority of the Dáil.

During the Dáil debates on the treaty, Childers spoke vigorously against acceptance. He was one of the most ardent and most vitriolic opponents of the treaty and concentrated on the defence clause of the document. His attitude in the Dáil alienated many former comrades and deepened the rift between himself and the pro-treaty side. He followed De Valera when the anti-Treatyites walked out of the Dáil, but became a marginal figure as politics were superseded by military action in the civil war that followed. When fighting broke out in Dublin, Childers found that he was a wanted man and fled the capital city, charging Molly and his family with the task of continuing to print Republican anti-treaty propaganda. However, when

Childers arrived in the southwest of Ireland, he found that the IRA brigades of Cork and Kerry did not trust him either. He was much older than most of the new generation of younger volunteers; he was an Englishman and an outsider, and his background in British intelligence was well known, as were the rumours alleging him to be a spy. Unpopular with the IRA, neither was Childers accepted by the Irish government who believed him to have played a key role in encouraging the anti-treaty military struggle. However, despite Childers' support for the Irregulars, it is unlikely that his contribution had any real impact on their military activities. He was certainly a supporter of that struggle, and there were rumours that Liam Lynch, the anti-treaty chief of staff, would have liked Childers to replace De Valera as leader of the political wing of the republicans. Such rumours also meant that the British government also detested Childers, viewing his conversion to the Irish cause as a horrid act of treachery. Options were running out for Childers!

The civil war was going badly for the Irregulars and Childers and his comrade David Robinson were involved in a dramatic and dangerous escape from the southwest. Avoiding the main roads, Childers made his way with difficulty to the remote fastnesses of the Wicklow Mountains, seeking refuge at Glendalough House, the home of his cousins, the Bartons. On 10 November 1922, the Barton house at Annamoe was raided and Childers was captured and imprisoned for possession of a small pearl-handled pistol. Ironically, the pistol had been a gift from pro-treaty leader Michael Collins. Childers, however, was put on trial for possession of a firearm, an offence punishable by death under the strict new Public Safety Act introduced by the Free State government. Animosity towards Childers was evident when he was publicly denounced in the Irish parliament by Kevin O'Higgins and in the English parliament by Winston Churchill. The Childers verdict was a foregone conclusion and on 24 November 1922, Robert Erskine Childers, the little English boy who had grown up in County Wicklow, was executed by an Irish firing squad.

Papers left by Childers suggest that his motivation for supporting the Irish cause was a wish to reconcile the differences between Ireland and Britain. However, his inflexible nature meant that his role in the treaty negotiations, the Dáil treaty debates and, to a lesser extent, the civil war was actually the opposite to his stated objective. This inflexibility alienated all sides, and Childers paid the ultimate price. After Erskine's death, Molly and the family remained in Ireland and did much to reconcile the pro- and anti-treaty sides after the Civil War. In 1973 their eldest son, Erskine Hamilton Childers, was elected president of the Ireland created by the treaty opposed so vehemently by his father – who would probably have been proud!

9

WICKLOW ON THE SILVER SCREEN

The magnificent scenery of Wicklow has meant that the county has featured in many movies, short films, commercials and television series through the years. In comparison to other Irish counties, Wicklow holds a unique place in movie history due to the number of major films made here. The breathtaking backdrop of wild rugged mountains, majestic waterfalls, golden beaches, remote glens and charming villages has acted like a magnet for many filmmakers. Some of the better-known movies of yesteryear include *Henry V*, *The Blue Max* and *Barry Lyndon*. It is no surprise that Ireland's principal film studio, Ardmore, is located in County Wicklow. A fine new studio, Ballyhenry, is also under construction in Ashford, close to Wicklow town.

Ardmore Studios, Bray, opened in 1958 and more than a hundred movies have been shot on location here and in the surrounding countryside. In the past, stars such as Fred Astaire, Richard Burton, Robert Mitchum, Peter O'Toole, Katharine Hepburn and Julie Andrews have graced the studios with their performances. More recently, actors of the calibre of Tom Cruise, Richard Dreyfuss, Ben Kingsley, Daniel Day Lewis, Liam Neeson, Morgan Freeman, Meryl Streep and Nicole Kidman have continued Wicklow's fine film tradition. The list of directors is equally impressive and includes names such as Francis Ford Coppola, John Boorman, Mel Gibson, Neil Jordan and David Lean.

Major awards have also come the way of Ardmore films, including Katharine Hepburn's Oscar for best actress (*The Lion in Winter*, 1968), and Daniel Day Lewis's best actor and Brenda Fricker's best supporting actress (*My Left Foot*, 1989). There were also the best director and best picture Oscars for Mel Gibson's *Braveheart* (1995). More recently, the television series *The Tudors* amassed a fine haul of Emmy awards too. Actors in many other Ardmore films have also been nominated for Academy Awards, including Richard Burton (*The Spy Who Came in from the Cold*), Peter O'Toole (*The Lion in Winter*) and Richard Harris (*The Field*), all of whom were nominated for best actor. Daniel Day Lewis, who won the best actor award in 1989, now lives in County Wicklow and was the first person to have been awarded the Freedom of County Wicklow for his contribution to international filmmaking and for the positive worldwide exposure that he has given to the county.

EXCALIBUR DRIVE

County Wicklow boasts no fewer than three dedicated movie drives, where fans can visit the sites made famous in each movie. The first of these is the Excalibur Drive. John Boorman's *Excalibur* was released in 1981. The film starred Liam Neeson, Gabriel Byrne, Helen Mirren, Cherie Lunghi and Nigel Terry. It concentrated on the fortunes of Arthur's magic sword, Excalibur, following its path through Arthurian myth. The forest scenes were shot within a mile of Boorman's Irish home. Filming also took place at Luggala estate, Powerscourt Waterfall, Childers Wood, Lough Tay and Wicklow Head. Igraine, the young Sir Mordred and the Lady of the Lake were all played by John Boorman's own children.

The Excalibur Drive starts in Ireland's highest village, Roundwood, and weaves its way through some of the most rugged scenery in Ireland as it climbs past Lough Tay towards the isolated and remote Sally Gap. From there it descends via Upper and Lower Lough Bray to Glencree, and continues through the heavily forested area around Powerscourt estate, taking in the magnificent waterfall used in many scenes in the film. The drive continues through Enniskerry and into Bray, the location of Ardmore studios. Bray's exquisite Killruddery House and gardens has also been used as a set for many films and television series. From Bray, the Excalibur Drive follows the coast via Greystones and Kilcoole. One has the option of continuing south to visit Wicklow Head, where the coastal scenes were filmed, but the route of the actual Excalibur Drive swings southwest from Kilcoole to Newtownmountkennedy, before climbing steeply towards Vartry Reservoir to finish once again in the pretty village of Roundwood. This route meanders through some of the highest mountains in Ireland. The rounded granite summits exceed 650 metres (*c.* 2,000 feet) in height, and contain the largest upland blanket bog in Ireland, much of it unspoiled and undisturbed. Wildlife thrives all along the 68-kilometre drive, and one may be lucky enough to spot deer, badgers, foxes, hedgehogs, falcons and, most appropriately, merlins in the upland regions.

BRAVEHEART DRIVE

The second County Wicklow film route is the Braveheart Drive. Mel Gibson's *Braveheart* first appeared on cinema screens in 1995, starring Brendan Gleeson, Patrick McGoohan, Sean McGinley, Sophie Marceau and Gibson himself. It tells the story of the Scottish patriot, William Wallace, and his attempts to resist English incursion into his homeland. Filming took place in west Wicklow in the area around Hollywood and Ballymore Eustace (in neighbouring County Kildare) as the rugged Wicklow Mountains around Kippure and the Sally Gap made a splendid backdrop for the historical epic. Mel Gibson decided to shoot the film in Wicklow when the Irish government offered him the use of the FCA (Irish army reservists) for the battle scenes. Horses were also needed, and an invitation was issued to all horse owners in the Wicklow and Kildare region to bring their mounts along and participate in these scenes as equine extras. The battle scenes were so realistic that the RSPCA launched an investigation, refusing to believe that the model horses used to portray battle injuries were not real. Gibson's assistant had to show the RSPCA investigators taped footage shot on location before they were persuaded that no cruelty to animals had taken place. The 80-kilometre Braveheart Drive begins in the appropriately named west Wicklow village of Hollywood, which was also used in the making of *Dancing at Lughnasa*. The road rises steeply before turning north towards Ballyknockan and on through Lackan, two incredibly picturesque villages overlooking the wide expanse of Blessington Lake. The route veers eastwards from Manor Kilbride, ascending via the Kippure estate through the virgin bog forming an extensive peatland, through which the headwaters of the Liffey flow as the famous river begins its winding journey towards the city of Dublin. Once the Sally Gap is reached, the journey continues via the spectacular Glenmacnass Waterfall to the ancient monastic site of Glendalough. Another climb brings one to the Wicklow Gap, passing by Lough Nahanagan and the Turlough Hill hydroelectric power station before the road descends back down to Hollywood. The Braveheart Drive is among the most spectacular anywhere in Ireland, and there is an abundance of wildlife, both flora and fauna, along its length.

MICHAEL COLLINS DRIVE

Michael Collins is a name more synonymous with Cork than with Wicklow, but, despite that, the 72-kilometre Michael Collins Drive is located squarely in east Wicklow. Directed by Neil Jordan, the 1996 film *Michael Collins* was one of the most successful movies ever released in Ireland. It starred Liam Neeson, Julia Roberts, Stephen Rea, Alan Rickman, Aidan Quinn and Sean McGinley. The movie deals with the life of the eponymous rebel, the man who is popularly perceived as being one of the principal leaders of the IRA during Ireland's War of

Independence, and the leader of the pro-treaty Free State army during the civil war that followed. The film received a PG rating from the Irish censor, despite being certified 'over 15' in many other countries because of its many scenes of violence and brutality. In Ireland though, the censor issued a statement in which he defended his decision to apply the PG rating, claiming that the movie was a landmark in Irish cinema. The statement went on to explain that he believed that 'because of the subject matter, parents should have the option of making their own decision as to whether their children should see the film or not'. The historical content and context of the film ensured that it was a huge box office success in Ireland, and much of it was shot on location in County Wicklow, in and around Hollywood, Bray, Rathdrum, Glenmalure, Glencree, Aghavannagh, Lough Dan and Greenan. The Michael Collins Drive concentrates on the south-eastern section of the county, and is unusual in that it does not pass through highland Wicklow. Instead, it brings one through an undulating landscape of rolling foothills and long verdant valleys containing picture-postcard villages. The route begins in Wicklow town and winds through Rathnew and Glenealy before reaching Rathdrum, where many scenes from the movie were shot. One continues to Avoca, scene of the Meeting of the Waters and well known to the many fans of *Ballykissangel*, a hugely successful television series, which was also filmed here. From Avoca it's on to Woodenbridge, where John Redmond's famous speech in 1914 ensured that over 200,000 Irishmen joined the British army during the First World War. The route then wends its way into the busy and historic seaport of Arklow before travelling through a rolling, hilly landscape to Redcross village and then on to the golden sands of the beach at Brittas Bay, which was used as a film location for *Camelot*, *The Count of Monte Cristo* and *The Tudors*. The drive continues along the east coast, finishing where it began in the county town of Wicklow.

It is fitting that County Wicklow contains a Michael Collins Drive because of the Big Fella's attitude to the people of the

Garden County. This is probably best encapsulated in the story of how a monument of Wicklow granite marks the birthplace of Michael Collins at Sam's Cross in County Cork. A deputation from the Collins memorial committee in Cork arrived in Wicklow's granite-quarrying village of Ballyknockan to procure the stone. They made it clear that only Wicklow granite would do for the monument, and when asked why, they said it was at the request of the sisters of Michael Collins. The Collins siblings said this was because, when Michael made his last visit home on the day before he was shot dead at Béal na mBláth, there was a house party to mark the occasion, during which the leader was asked: 'You've been all over Ireland and met people from every county; which of them do you like the best?' Collins answered straightaway: 'The people from the County Wicklow'. In the movie, the ambush at Béal na mBláth was filmed on the road near the village of Hollywood.

HOLLYWOOD

This Wicklow Hollywood is much older than its American counterpart. The original name was actually Holy Wood, and this form of the name, *Sanctum Nemus* in Latin, was recorded in Norman records in the year 1192. The Irish version of the name, *Cillín Chaoimhín* (Kevin's little church), was also noted in 1192. St Kevin, the patron saint of County Wicklow, came to Hollywood to seek sanctuary and solitude from the outside world. As mentioned earlier, legend has it that a lady named Kathleen, who had designs on the saint, followed him here, so he crossed the Wicklow Mountains, arriving at the even more remote site of Glendalough, where he lived as a hermit, and where a monastic site developed later on. St Kevin may have left Hollywood behind him, but he gave his name to the village of the holy wood, which is still known as *Cillín Chaoimhín* in the Irish language. Today, many tourists come to Hollywood every year and are fascinated that such a small village can share its name with somewhere as famous as

Tinseltown, USA. They often take photographs in the village, especially at the post office, where the name 'Hollywood' is prominently displayed over the door. They would be even more fascinated – flabbergasted in fact – if they knew the truth. This Hollywood in Wicklow was actually the original after which its more famous namesake in California was named. A nineteenth-century post-Famine emigrant from Wicklow's Hollywood, Matthew Guirke, became a successful businessman in California. He was the owner of a racetrack, and he bought land in the now famous suburb of Los Angeles, naming it Hollywood after his native place back in Ireland. Matthew Guirke was an ancestor of Jim Guirke, who ran the post office in Wicklow's Hollywood until he passed away in 2003, so the tourists taking the pictures outside were actually a lot more closely linked with Hollywood USA than they ever imagined.

FAMOUS FILMS

County Wicklow may not quite match Hollywood USA in the number of films produced, but in the Irish context the Garden County remains at the head of the pack in terms of quantity over the past quarter of a century or so. In 1989 director Jim Sheridan's Irish classic, *My Left Foot*, was shot at locations including Ardmore Studios, Wicklow Head and Bray. This poignant film tells the story of disabled Irish author Christy Brown, who suffered from cerebral palsy and was believed to be mentally retarded during the first 10 years of his life. Brown could only speak by means of guttural sounds, clicks and grunts and struggled to survive in the midst of a working-class Irish family. However, through the good work of a remarkable teacher and the persistence of his mother, the youth learned to control the movement of his left foot in order to paint, and write poetry and stories. The inspirational Christy Brown left a valuable legacy of literature; his best-known work was *Down All the Days*, which was published in 1970. Daniel Day Lewis's moving portrayal of the author and the resulting Oscar was the catalyst for the production of a wide range of films in Wicklow during the 1990s.

In 1992 Mike Newell's fantasy *Into the West* was released. This surreal adventure starred Gabriel Byrne, Colm Meaney, Brendan Gleeson and Ellen Barkin. Parts of the film were shot along Bray's Quinsboro Road, and the Luggala estate was extensively used to film the rural shots as Ossie and Tato embark on their big adventure. The highland area of the Wicklow Mountains also provided spectacular backdrops, including Turlough Hill, the Wicklow Gap and Powerscourt Waterfall, as their journey unfolded. Aerial camera work was done around Inchinappa near Ashford. The film became a modern Irish classic.

Another Wicklow-filmed Irish classic hit our screens in 1998 with the release of Pat O'Connor's *Dancing at Lughnasa*. With an all-star cast including Meryl Streep and Michael Gambon, the movie was shot at locations including Hollywood, Kippure estate, Luggala estate, the Sally Gap and Lough Dan. The cottage seen in the film was specially built in Coronation Plantation near the Sally Gap. Based on Brian Friel's play of the same name, the movie follows the fortunes of the Mundy family, dealing with themes such as family and religion set in the grinding poverty of 1930s Ireland. Despite the grim storyline, the movie was a box office success and attracted much critical acclaim.

There was critical acclaim also for *Ballykissangel*, filmed in Wicklow between 1996 and 2001. Although the series will always be associated with Avoca, where the village scenes were shot, filming also took place at Roundwood, Ballysmuttan Bridge, Glencree, Bray, Enniskerry, Brittas Bay, Wicklow Head and Luggala estate. The cast included Stephen Tomkinson, Dervla Kirwan, Colin Farrell, Victoria Smurfit and Niall Toibin. Avoca became a Mecca for fans of the series and the many visitors greatly helped the local economy. Fitzgerald's public house, the local shops, the Garda station and the church were all must-see items on the list of visiting Ballykissangel aficionados. By the time the series finished in 2001, it had helped to establish Wicklow even more as a movie location, and, as the twenty-first century dawned, the film floodgates opened with a plethora of movies and television series emanating from the county from then onwards.

Directed by Kevin Reynolds, *The Count of Monte Cristo* was released in 2002 and is a remake of the Alexander Dumas novel. Dantes, a sailor who is falsely accused of treason, is imprisoned for 13 years. However, he escapes and uses hidden treasure to become the Count of Monte Cristo, and to plot his revenge. Starring James Caviezel, Richard Harris and Guy Pearce, scenes were shot at Silver Strand (where Dantes is washed ashore after his escape from the Chateau d'If prison), Brittas Bay, Blainroe Beach, Killruddery House, Enniskerry and Powerscourt House, where Dantes, as the count, made his new home. Wicklow also became home to dragons in 2002, when Rob Bowman's *Reign of Fire* was shown in cinemas for the first time. Its cast included Christian Bale, Izabella Scorupco, Matthew McConaughey and Gerard Butler. A futuristic tale of dragons and human survivors in a post-apocalyptic world, the movie was shot at locations including the Sally Gap, the Wicklow Gap, Ballinascorney Quarry and the Black Castle in Wicklow town. A large castle was erected for the film at the head of the Glendasan valley, in the heart of the Wicklow Mountains National Park. Such was the environmental sensitivity of this site that a huge synthetic membrane was used to cover the entire site before filming began, and in order to help with the restoration of the site once the project was finished. The restoration was a complete success, so environmentally, as well as on-screen, good won out in the battle over evil!

The battle between good and evil again featured in 2004 when Antoine Fuqua's *King Arthur*, another remake of the Arthurian legend covering much of the same ground as *Excalibur*, was released. The cast included Owen Wilson, Kiera Knightly and Ray Winstone and the opening scenes were shot at Turlough Hill and the Wicklow Gap. A massive replica of Hadrian's Wall was erected in the Ballymore Eustace-Hollywood area of west Wicklow, and Hollywood Glen was covered with fake snow for the frozen lake sequence. Many of the battle scenes were also filmed in west Wicklow. Fraughan Rock Glen and Glenmalure were used to film the journey scenes and a replica Roman villa and village were specially erected in Glenmalure. Roundwood and the enchanting Luggala also featured in the movie.

Enchantment of another kind was also created in Wicklow in 2004, with the release of *Ella Enchanted*. Directed by Tommy O'Haver and starring Anne Hathaway, Hugh Dancy, Minnie Driver, Cary Elwes, Heidi Klum and Joanna Lumley, and based on Carson Levine's 1997 novel, the film is a fairy tale in which Ella is under the influence of a spell that makes her always obedient. However, she cannot let her step-family know about this spell, nor can she reveal it to her friend the prince, who is perhaps becoming more than just a friend. Filming for this movie was done in Powerscourt House and gardens, Killruddery House and gardens, and Enniskerry.

The year 2005 saw another children's film produced in Wicklow hit the cinema screens, when Charles Sturridge's *Lassie* was released. The cast included Peter O'Toole, Samantha Morton and John Lynch, but the real star was the collie, Lassie. This was a remake of an earlier classic and Luggala estate, Killruddery House and gardens, and Roundwood all featured, with much aerial camera work over the Wicklow Mountains as Lassie embarked on her adventurous journey to find her way home.

No fewer than three major films came out of Wicklow in 2007. Directed by Richard LaGravenese, *P.S. I Love You* is based on a novel by Cecilia Aherne, daughter of former Irish prime minister, Taoiseach Bertie Aherne. Starring Hilary Swank and Gerard Butler, the film follows the heroine on a journey from New York to Ireland. Scenes were shot mainly in west Wicklow. The scene where Holly and Gerry meet for the first time is at the Sally Gap, and the 'Dun Laoghaire' scene was filmed at Lackan on Blessington Lake. Roundwood was also used as a location in this film and in Julian Jarrold's *Becoming Jane*, which starred Anne Hathaway and James McAvoy. The opening sequence of this period drama was shot at Wicklow courthouse, and the picnic scene was at Luggala estate. The Anglican church and Cloghleagh bridge at Manor Kilbride were also used in the movie. The third film to emerge from County Wicklow in 2007 was the poignant First World War drama *My Boy Jack*. Directed by Brian Kirk and starring Daniel Radcliffe, David Haig, Carey Mulligan and Kim Cattrall, the film follows the fortunes of the eponymous hero, with Clermont College in Rathnew providing an excellent location for both the War Office and the hospital scenes. Battle scenes were shot in trenches on a farm in Ashford and Ardmore studios were also used to recreate the historical atmosphere of the time.

In addition to three major films, the year 2007 also saw the beginning of another major historical television series shot on location in Wicklow. *The Tudors* received many Golden Globe nominations and won many Emmy Awards. Featuring a cast that included Jonathan Rhys-Meyers, Peter O'Toole, Natalie Dormer, Henry Cavill, James Frain and Maria Doyle-Kennedy, the series enjoyed astronomical viewing figures during the 4 years of filming in Wicklow. Killruddery House and gardens, Powerscourt House and gardens, Luggala estate, Humewood Castle, Grange farm near Newcastle, Brennanstown Riding School near Bray and Lough Dan all provided locations for filming. The series employed in excess of 200 cast and crew members and used over 1,500 extras, which provided a huge boost to Ireland's film industry and had a massive economic spin-off in County Wicklow. *The Tudors* centres on King Henry VIII, who has his hands full trying to stave off

court plots and political intrigue while facing major threats from foreign powers and trying to beget a male heir – which leads to conflict with the pope, a divorce from Catherine of Aragon and ultimately the Henrician Reformation in England. Catherine's successor as Henry's wife, Anne Boleyn, also failed to produce a male heir, so she was beheaded and Henry subsequently married Jane Seymour, Anne of Cleves, Catherine Howard and Catherine Parr before his death. Historical drama, lots of love interest and a Wicklow backdrop – no wonder the series was a smash hit!

Love interest was once again apparent when Anand Tucker's *Leap Year* was released in 2010. Principals Amy Adams, Matthew Goode and Adam Scott become involved in a love triangle when the heroine follows the man of her dreams to Ireland, inspired by the old Irish tradition that a lady can (and should) propose to her man during a leap year. However, she lands on the wrong side of Ireland and has to cross the country in the company of another man, a journey on which she finds that one's dreams may

change! Filming took place at Glendalough, the Glen of Imaal, Enniskerry, Roundwood and Luggala.

Luggala was also used in the 2011 television series *Camelot*. The cast included Clive Standen, Tasmin Egerton, Joseph Fiennes, Eva Green and Jamie Campbell Bower. Shot at many Wicklow locations including Killruddery, Powerscourt, Brittas Bay, Magheramore Beach and Roundwood, the series is a retelling of the Arthurian legend, though perhaps with a darker twist than the other Arthurian movies shot in the county. The scenery of County Wicklow lends itself as a backdrop to heroic tales, and it is fitting that *Camelot*, one of the latest offerings to come out of the county, covers similar ground to *Excalibur*, the film that really began Wicklow's modern film boom. Today, that boom is continuing, and Ardmore Studios are currently busily working on more movies, television series, one-off programmes and commercials, while shooting on location is also taking place for various projects. At the time of writing, the television series *The Vikings* is being shot in Wicklow, so the unsuspecting visitor should not be too surprised to see fearsome Norse longships on Blessington Lake. With a new state-of-the-art studio coming on stream at Ballyhenry, the prospects for County Wicklow's film industry – complete with its own version of Hollywood – looks set to remain rosy well into the future.

10

WICKLOW'S HISTORIC TOWNS

Any tourist in Wicklow is spoilt for choice when it comes to urban settlements to visit. Whether vibrant large towns or charming smaller ones, these places all have a character of their own. The land at the centre of the county is very rugged and altitude discourages the building of towns, so the county's more sizeable settlements are to be found in the east, along the low-lying fertile coastal plain. There are also some smaller towns in the lower lands of west Wicklow. Whether large or small, east or west, all of them are steeped in history and this chapter gives a brief outline of the history and heritage associated with some of Wicklow's principal towns.

ARKLOW

A town of great antiquity, Arklow was known to the second-century Greek geographer Ptolemy of Alexandria. Situated on the coast and with a fine harbour, it was probably a point of entry and exit for many traders. It was also a point of entry for the Vikings, who plundered the Irish coast from the ninth to the eleventh centuries but also settled in coastal areas, founding and building towns; Arklow was a Viking fishing settlement. Following the Norman invasion of 1169, the building of a castle meant that the town became an important centre of defence. In 1396 King Richard II used Arklow as a base from which to subdue the warlike Irish clans in the surrounding region. Unsurprisingly, the town had a boat-building industry and developed as a fishing port, and there are references to fishing grounds off Arklow in medieval documents. Part of the town became known as 'The Fishery' and was shown in two distinct parts (town and fishery) on later maps.

Arklow was the scene of a large and fierce battle during the 1798 rebellion. Thousands of rebels moved north from Wexford on 9 June to attack Arklow, which was defended by about 1,500 government troops under General Francis Needham. The resulting hard-fought battle lasted for many hours, and the rebels eventually retreated, having failed to take the town but having ensured that about a third of Needham's force became casualties. For days afterwards, over a thousand rebel corpses were left to rot in the streets before they were buried in mass graves in the Ferrybank area of the town (then an unoccupied site).

The town grew rapidly during the nineteenth century and Arklow was the location of Ireland's first lifeboat station, but the century's later decades saw the beginning of the long and protracted decline of the fishing industry. The Fishery area experienced urban deterioration and later twentieth-century urban regeneration as other industries were established. Kynochs' factory made munitions during the First World War, and continued in operation after the conflict. In November 1920, at the height of the War of Independence, the IRA carried out a raid on Kynochs' and escaped with a quantity of explosives. Andrew Kavanagh recalled that 'we raided the old site of Kynochs' and got 25 cwt of TNT, in an incomplete form – this, despite the fact the military had patrols all over the town. We put it on a car, and it was conveyed to Dublin'. These explosives were later used in several IRA attacks around the country. When peace returned and an independent Ireland emerged, Arklow was later known for its pottery and fertiliser industries. The fine nineteen-arch bridge is the longest of its type in Ireland. Today, Arklow Maritime Museum recalls the town's seafaring past and many other aspects of its history.

AUGHRIM

Aughrim's strategic location at the convergence of many mountain valleys classifies it as a gap town and a nodal point, commanding many routes radiating outwards from its centre. It is also a river crossing point. Nicknamed the 'Granite City', many of the buildings utilise the local stone, which sparkles magnificently in the sunshine. The core of the town contains many fine old buildings including two churches, a mill, a hotel, a forge, a market house and a number of impressive town houses. The functions of some of these buildings have changed over time, but they add greatly to the old-world atmosphere in the central area, where there is also a fine monument to commemorate the 1798 rebellion. Aughrim suffered badly during this time and was reduced to a burnt-out shell before peace was restored. Today the forestry industry has become important in the Aughrim region, but the town is perhaps best known as the headquarters of the Wicklow GAA and the location of the county grounds, where Wicklow's Gaelic footballers play their home games.

AVOCA

Although too small to qualify as a town, Avoca is a must-visit destination for many visitors to Wicklow. Known to millions as 'Ballykissangel' from the BBC television series, the village of Avoca is also associated with Thomas Moore, once known as Ireland's national poet. The poet Thomas Moore was born in Dublin on 28 May 1779, and his *Irish Melodies* were published between 1807 and 1834. One of his best-known works concerns Avoca and begins with the lines:

> There is not in this wide world a valley so sweet
> As the vale in whose bosom the bright waters meet
>
> (Thomas Moore, *The Meeting of the Waters*, 1808)

Moore penned the poem on a rustic seat formed from the root of an old oak tree, and it goes on to describe the beauties of Avoca. The tree, known now as Tom Moore's tree, still exists at the confluence of the Avonmore and Avonbeg rivers just outside Avoca. It is probable that 'Oboca' on Ptolemy's map refers to Avoca. There are records of many ancient churches here, but the Roman Catholic church of Saints Mary and Patrick dates from 1862 and the Church of Ireland church of the Holy Trinity was consecrated on 27 April 1870. Over a thousand men were employed in the copper mines here in the 1840s. Avoca was also the scene of a gold rush in the late eighteenth century; one 22-ounce nugget was made into a snuff box for King George III. A mineral tramway was constructed to bring the copper ore to Arklow during the Great Famine, and the labour required for this project saved many local people from destitution and starvation. Today, the spot is a major tourist attraction, and visitors also call in to the Avoca Handweavers' store. The core of the village contains a mill, a courthouse, two churches and a school, some of which have lost their former functions.

BALTINGLASS

The heritage town of Baltinglass is at the centre of west Wicklow, and for many centuries was regarded as the most significant settlement in that part of the county. The town's origins are lost in the mists of antiquity. The Iron Age settlement at nearby Spinan's Hill is one of the largest and most important of its kind in the British Isles. The ruined Cistercian abbey at the centre of the town was founded in 1148 and was one of very few abbeys to pre-date the Norman invasion. However, when Norman monks were installed there, it became a target for native Irish raids and ceased to be an abbey when King Henry VIII dissolved the monasteries. The powerful Stratford family settled here and controlled the area in the eighteenth century. One of the most famous inhabitants of Baltinglass was Richard Crosbie (1756–1824), who was the first Irish balloonist. He constructed a hydrogen balloon and over 20,000 people gathered at Ranelagh Gardens, Dublin, to witness the first successful manned flight in Ireland. Crosbie made three subsequent flights, two in Dublin and one in Limerick, before he moved to America, where he became an actor in New York.

Baltinglass was a military base during the 1798 rebellion and many rebels were court-martialled and executed in the town. A wall plaque on the site of the old gaol commemorates them. Another famous native of Baltinglass was John O'Brien, who witnessed the 1798 violence as a boy. By 1812 the young John O'Brien had arrived in Buenos Aires – the unknown Baltinglass youth was on his way to becoming the South American legend General John Thomond O'Brien. His contribution to the independence movements in many South American countries, including Argentina and Chile, is immense by any standards. O'Brien was involved in the independence movements in five South American states and held commissions in

three armies. In later life he undertook diplomatic missions to establish relations between these states and Europe. He died in Lisbon in 1861. A wall plaque in the historic centre of Baltinglass recalls his deeds. Another wall plaque honours Jenny Wyse Power (1858–1941), probably the best-known daughter of Baltinglass and a leading figure in the feminist and suffrage struggles of the late nineteenth and early twentieth centuries. She was involved in public life from her youth and was an ardent nationalist. She played an active part in the 1916 Easter Rising and in the subsequent conflict that led to the establishment of the Irish Free State. She was a senator in the Irish government for nearly 14 years and was a voice for women's issues throughout that time. There is also a statue of Sam McAllister, a 1798 rebel, in the centre of Baltinglass.

BLESSINGTON

The area around Blessington was settled in ancient times, and the charter establishing a town here was granted to Michael Boyle (later to become Primate Bishop of Armagh) in 1667. The Boyles became Viscounts of Blessington and the market town prospered. Rebels encamped near the town in 1798 and Blessington House, which by then had passed from the Boyle family to the Hills, Marquises of Downshire, was burned down. The town recovered and a fine market square at its centre testifies to its function as a market town. Blessington fared badly during the Famine, and a unique primary source gives an account of the day-to-day life here during the Famine years. This is the diary of Mrs Elizabeth Smith, a Scottish woman who had married Henry Smith of Baltiboys House, Blessington. She recorded the first instance of potato blight on 26 October 1845. The situation rapidly deteriorated and on 25 September 1846 Elizabeth wrote: 'Here comes the Famine ... the rain has spoiled the few miserable potatoes left ... so here we are, the peasantry starving'. In Christmas week 1846 she observed: 'The Famine has come [to] every neglected property ... the poorhouse is full, 1,100 where there never was 200'. On 7 April 1850 she was almost in despair as emigration levels soared in an attempt to escape the Famine: 'Crowds upon crowds swarm along the roads, the bye roads, following carts with their trunks and other property'. Fortunately, Blessington survived, albeit with a smaller population.

A steam tram link was opened between Dublin and Blessington, improving communication links with the capital. The line was reputed to be 'the longest graveyard in Ireland' because of the number of roadside memorials erected to those who had been killed by its trams. Many accidents occurred due to the lack of staff training, the lack of safety awareness, the poor quality of both the tracks and their bed, the open-topped tram, the rural route and the amounts of alcohol consumed by both rural visitors to Dublin and urban day-trippers to Wicklow! The tracks ran along Blessington's main street until the closure of the line in 1932. A decade previously, Blessington was the scene of one of the first battles of the Irish Civil War. Irregulars who opposed the Anglo-Irish Treaty gathered in the town. They expected to reinforce their

comrades in Dublin, but they engaged with Free State army forces and IRA commander Oscar Traynor made it clear that the Irregulars were beaten in the capital, so they retreated from Blessington, with many of them, such as IRA leader Ernie O'Malley, continuing the fight in Munster. In the late twentieth century, urban sprawl in Dublin saw many suburbs and new towns such as Tallaght spring up west of Dublin, effectively reducing the distance between Blessington and Ireland's capital city. Blessington became a desirable location as a dormitory town and grew quickly. Despite rapid growth, the town retains its charming historic core and St Mary's Church of Ireland church, dating from 1683, still has its original peal of bells. With its adjacent lake (a man-made reservoir on the River Liffey, which has been dammed above the old waterfall at Poulaphuca), Blessington remains an attractive destination for visitors.

BRAY

For many years the largest town in County Wicklow, Bray was a vibrant, historic urban settlement. There is evidence of Bronze Age settlement here, but the town developed around the manor granted to the Norman Walter de Ridelesford *c.* 1171. De Ridelesford was one of the principal followers of Strongbow (Richard de Clare, Earl of Pembroke) who led the Norman invasion of Ireland. The original settlement had a castle, church and mill, and in 1619 King James I granted Killruddery House to the Brabazon family,

whose presence regenerated the town. Bray remained a small settlement though until the nineteenth century. In the 1830s work began on a railway line in Bray, but obstacles soon presented themselves. The construction of the railway line so close to the coast necessitated the building of a bridge over the River Dargle, the reclamation of land on the seaward side of the bridge and the creation of a long embankment to the south of the river. A new dock also had to be built to accommodate the boats that had previously moored in the river estuary. Despite these difficulties, the railway line from Dublin to Bray was formally opened on 10 July 1854. Bray's proximity to Dublin made it the ideal destination for a day trip to the beach. It quickly gained a reputation as a seaside resort, and became known as 'the Brighton of Ireland'. The town mushroomed, with hotels and guesthouses springing up all along the seafront and the smaller streets joining it to the town's Main Street. These fine Victorian and Edwardian buildings still stand today and contribute to the unique and charming character of the town. A fine esplanade was built behind the beach, just right for Victorians to promenade and take the sea air! This is backed by grassy areas with kiosks and bandstands, adding to the feeling of spaciousness in this part of the town. Bray remained one of Ireland's premier holiday destinations for a century or so, and still receives a large number of visitors, many of whom now use Dublin's commuter rail link, the DART, to access the town.

The most prominent public building in Bray is the town hall and market house, which stands at the top of Main Street. This Victorian Neo-Gothic gem was the brainchild of Reginald and Mary Brabazon. The Brabazons gave the task of designing it to a firm of leading Irish architects, Thomas Newenham Deane & Son. Deane was the son of Sir Thomas Deane, the noted Cork architect, but the design of Bray's town hall and market house is actually the work of Edward Guy Dawber, a young assistant in Deane's office. The Main Street façade is tall, slim and elegant, but the sides are elongated. The façade's central arch boasts very intricate wrought-iron gates, dated 1881. The building's transom and mullioned windows are based on the windows of Sparrowe's House in Ipswich. The market house was once at the centre of commerce in Bray, and the building dominates the top of Main Street, which is now a busy centre of trade and commerce in its own right. Population growth during the late twentieth century has continued in Bray, ensuring that this historic seaside town has a bright future as well as an interesting past.

GREYSTONES

Built on a rocky outcrop to the south of Bray Head, Greystones has a long history but developed primarily as a fishing village. In 1795 *Topographia Hibernica* stated that 'Greystones is a noted fishing village four miles beyond Bray. The herrings first brought into Dublin are usually taken by the fishing boats of this place'. In 1801 Greystones was described as 'a fine natural harbour and an excellent roadstead for ships of any burden from fishing vessels to the largest frequenting the seas'. Like Arklow, the town has a boat-building tradition and boats made by Greystones shipwrights gained a reputation of being lucky vessels. As the nineteenth century progressed, a jetty was built at the northern end of Greystones to facilitate the local fishing boats. The development of the fishing industry was only one aspect of the growth of Greystones; however, in 1753 David La Touche purchased a country estate and commissioned the building of Belleview House. The La Touches would become prominent in the town's history, and it was during the lifetime of William Robert La Touche, who succeeded to the estate in 1856, that Greystones really began to change. This was due in large part to the building of the railway between 1854 and 1856. No less a person than the famous British engineer, Isambard Kingdom Brunel, was called in to devise a way to bring the railway to the south of Bray Head. Although it meant the creation of many tunnels and much work on the seaward side of the headland, Brunel managed to run a single line along the difficult stretch. At Greystones the line ran along the boundary of the La Touche and Whitshed (another leading local family) estates, indicating that a compromise was made between their rival claims. Two new roads were also built at this time: one from the pier to the railway station and the other from the station towards the harbour. The growth of the town was also a factor in the opening of a new Church of Ireland church, which was consecrated on 19 July 1864. A Roman Catholic church was also built at this time, but it was replaced in 1909. The railway link increased the popularity of Greystones as a dormitory village for Dublin, but the line and some areas of the town were constantly under threat from marine erosion. The Irish Sea washed away land on the seaward side of the railway line even before 1900, and in 1917 a new tunnel was constructed further inland. This tunnel is some three-quarters of a mile long and is the second longest of its type in Ireland (the longest is in Cork).

The power of the sea often led to tragedy in Greystones. On 14 October 1892, three men went on to the pier during a violent storm to release the moorings of a schooner called *The Mersey*. All three were swept away by a huge wave. The appalled townspeople could do nothing as the men drowned within a few yards of dry land. In October 1911 three schooners – the *Vellenhellie*, the *Reciprocity* and the *Federation* – were all wrecked while moored at the pier in Greystones during another violent storm. These shipwrecks ensured that no insurance company would insure any ship in Greystones, and this led to the decline and demise of the harbour. The cruel sea did not confine its energy to ships. In 1928 a great storm meant that over thirty houses had to be evacuated and permanently vacated in Greystones as the sea took its inexorable toll. Today, the battle with the sea seems to have been won and much work has been done to make the old pier safe and the seafront attractive for visitors, many of whom take the train from the capital to visit this pleasant seaside town, which continues to grow due to its proximity to Dublin.

WICKLOW

The Irish name for Wicklow is Cill Mhantáin, which means Mantain's church. Mantain was a follower of St Patrick, who got the nickname Maintain (meaning gap-toothed) when natives of County Wicklow stoned Patrick and his followers when they first tried to land in Ireland in AD 432. They eventually got ashore and Patrick was very successful in converting the Irish to Christianity. He told Mantain to establish a church in Wicklow and oral tradition places this church between the town's courthouse and the corner of New Street and Main Street. In 1935, when excavation was carried out in this area, large slab stones were found and the foundations of large pre-Norman buildings were discovered, so the site may be the correct one. The English word 'Wicklow', on the other hand, is Norse in origin. It comes from a combination of two words, 'Vyk' and 'Lo', and translates as 'Meadow of the Vikings', although some etymologists argue the case for 'Bay of the Meadow'. Either way, it is certain that Wicklow town was a Viking settlement.

It developed as a port on Ireland's east coast and following the Norman invasion, Maurice Fitzgerald, the Norman Baron of Naas, built a castle here. The Black Castle, as it is known, is situated on a rocky headland and is separated from the mainland by an artificial fosse. The first reference to the castle dates from 1174, when it was mentioned in a grant made by King Henry II. The castle was to play a prominent role in the history of Wicklow town until the seventeenth century. The position of the Norman town and its low-lying site made it vulnerable to attacks from Irish clans such as the O'Byrnes and the O'Tooles, who had their strongholds in the Wicklow Mountains. Wicklow was attacked and burned in 1301 and 1315, and Norman power declined as the fourteenth century progressed. As the raids of the Irish succeeded and they dominated the area, the castle was neglected and began to fall into disrepair. In 1543 however, the Irish clans surrendered Wicklow and its castle to King Henry VIII, as the fortunes of war had swung back in England's favour. There were further attacks on the town and the castle, but the defeat of the Wicklow clans during the Nine Years' War of 1594–1603 meant that their lands were shired into a new county.

In 1606 County Wicklow became the last county to be created in Ireland. Wicklow town became the county town and soon took on administrative functions in fields such as local government and law and order. The 1641 rebellion saw the castle besieged by Luke O'Toole's forces, but Sir Charles Coote and his troops relieved the castle garrison. Coote's men carried out a horrendous massacre of Wicklow's inhabitants in a street still known as Melancholy Lane. However, another attack on the castle occurred in 1645 and this time the building was razed to the ground. It was never fully rebuilt – a partial restoration was neglected and the castle went into terminal decline. In the eighteenth century, the ruin and its lands were given to the portreeve for the benefit of the borough. The castle is almost totally obliterated, but its ruin forms part of a very scenic coastal route with hidden bays and coves and the Wicklow lighthouse along the way. In the town centre, a statue of 1798 rebel leader Billy Byrne of Ballymanus stands close to the old prison. Wicklow's historic gaol dominates this section of the town, but there are other fine public buildings in Wicklow such as the courthouse and churches. The pier and harbour area and its old warehouses indicate past industry and commerce, and the town is still a working port with a long-standing seafaring tradition.

Perhaps the best-known Wicklow seafarer was Captain Robert Halpin, whose birth here on 17 February 1836 is recorded on an obelisk in the town. Halpin was the youngest of thirteen children and first went to sea at the tender age of 11. He worked his way up through the ranks and 1865 saw him aboard the *Great Eastern*. This was the greatest ship of its day, a behemoth of 22,000 tons which was chartered to lay the first transatlantic telegraph cable between Ireland and Newfoundland. In 1866 Halpin was promoted to First Officer and, in 1868, to captain of the *Great Eastern*. He oversaw the completion of the transatlantic link and subsequently connected other continents by telegraph, laying some 26,000 miles of cable. The Victorians celebrated his achievements, and it is the Victorian character of the architecture in the historic core of Wicklow town that enhances its charm today.